Can't Stop Talking

Second Edition

Discussion Problems for Advanced Beginners and Low Intermediates

George Rooks

English for Foreign Students Program
University of California at Davis

HEINLE & HEINLE PUBLISHERS
A Division of Wadsworth, Inc.
Boston, Massachusetts 02116

Director: Laurie E. Likoff
Production Coordinator: Cynthia Funkhouser
Production: R. David Newcomer Associates
Text Design: Ron Newcomer
Cover Design/Adaptation: Catherine Gallagher
Copy Editor: Elliot Simon
Photo Research: Robin Risque
Compositor: TypeLink, Inc.
Printer and Binder: Malloy Lithographing, Inc.

Can't Stop Talking: Discussion Problems for Advanced Beginners and Low Intermediates, Second Edition

ISBN 0-8384-2914-9

Photo credits: Units 2 & 3, © 1989 Brian J. Berman; Unit 4, UN Photo 148693/Yutaka Negata; Unit 5, © B. G. Irwin; Unit 6, courtesy NASA; Unit 7, © 1988 Brian J. Berman; Unit 8, © Skjold Photographs; Unit 9, photo courtesy of the Beverly, Mass., *TIMES*; Unit 10, © B. G. Irwin; Unit 11, © Hearst Monument/Ken Raveill; Unit 12, © Reuters/Bettmann Newsphotos; Unit 13, United Way of America photo; Unit 14, © Skjold Photographs; Unit 15, © Arvind Garg 1989; Unit 16, courtesy OMNI Hotel, San Diego; Unit 17, © B. G. Irwin; Unit 18, courtesy of American Airlines; Unit 19, © B. G. Irwin; Unit 20, National Park Service, Department of the Interior; Unit 21, Washington Convention and Visitors' Association; Unit 22, © Alinari/Art Resource; Unit 23, photo courtesy of the Beverly, Mass., *TIMES*; Unit 24, © Camerique Stock Photos; Unit 25, (top left) © Arvind Garg 1989, (top right) © Jim Cox, the Salk Institute, (bottom left) © UPI/Bettmann Newsphotos, (bottom right) courtesy Mr. Abdul-Jabbar; Unit 26, © Skjold Photographs; Unit 27, courtesy of the United Nations; Unit 28, © Skjold Photographs; Unit 29, © Arvind Garg 1984; Unit 30, UN Photo 155748/Milton Grant; Unit 31, courtesy of the National Mine Service Company.

Library of Congress Cataloging-in-Publication Data

Rooks, George.
    Can't stop talking.

    1. English language—Textbooks for foreign speakers.   I. Title.
PE1128.R639   1989   428.3′4   89-13157

20 19 18 17 16 15 14 13 12 11 10

Contents

Your job is to interview tourists who have come to the United States. How can you find out their name? country? reason for coming? length of stay? Extend this exercise by interviewing one of your classmates and writing a composition about her or him.

You work for a dating service. You must match men and women together. Should the truck driver date the model? Should the karate teacher date the police officer? Extend this unit by discussing your attitudes toward dating.

You are members of a jury deciding the fate of six criminals. What should be the punishment for a drunk driver who runs over a child? for a man who steals bicycles for his children's Christmas presents? Extend this unit by considering, "Is it ever okay to steal?"

You are members of the Michigan legislature. You are trying to reduce the number of drunk-driving accidents. At what age should people be allowed to drive? What should be the penalty for drunk driving? Extend this discussion by considering which drugs are the most dangerous.

Your network needs new programs to try to win back its audience. What programs will attract the most viewers: nighttime soap operas? dramas? a cooking show? art? Extend by discussing whether government should control the programs we see on TV.

Your job is to design a fabulous new house for a wealthy client. Where will you put the swimming pool? six bedrooms? three fireplaces? tennis court? Extend by describing your parents' house as well as bringing to class pictures of your country's buildings.

You are members of the International Olympic Committee. Which cities will you choose as permanent winter and summer Olympic cities? Which 25 events will you choose to have? Extend this unit by organizing a competition in your class.

Which programs in the State of California do you think should receive state funding—and how much? a senior citizens' center? a pay raise for the legislature? jobs for unemployed teenagers? more police cars? Extend this problem by discussing whether it is better to have a large or small government.

Acknowledgments

First, I would like to thank Elizabeth Lantz for her untiring help with my series of texts, beginning with *The Non-Stop Discussion Workbook*, continuing with the current *Can't Stop Talking*, and branching out into the subsequent French, Spanish, and German adaptations. Without her great enthusiasm and her careful editing of manuscripts, I am sure, the series would not have been possible.

I am especially grateful to Beryl Duffin for giving me the independence in the classroom to produce such a book.

In the preparation of this edition, I particularly thank my wife, Hila, for her inspiration, ideas, and support.

Finally, I dedicate this workbook to my grandfather, who taught me the power of words.

George Rooks
University of California, Davis

To the Teacher

The purpose of this second edition of *Can't Stop Talking* is the same as that of the first: to create discussion or conversation situations in which the students do almost all the talking.

To accomplish this, the students receive a stimulating problem to solve and a straightforward method for solving it. Most of the problems pose serious and challenging dilemmas, ranging from budget decisions to a life-and-death situation. They also deal with a wide variety of subjects, to appeal to as many students as possible.

Each problem is presented through a combination of photograph/artwork and text. The photograph/artwork sets the scene. Each unit then consists of five sections: Vocabulary, Read and Consider, Decide and Write, Discuss, Extend. The Vocabulary section helps the developing student assimilate more words and better understand the unit. The Read and Consider section introduces the problem and sets out some of the factors to be weighed in the problem-solving process. The Decide and Write section gives guidelines for reaching a decision. The Discuss section then directs the students to compare verbally the decisions they have made. Finally, the Extend section attempts to expand each student's thinking beyond the often-nonjudgmental result of values clarification.

These problems work best when the discussion groups have from four to six students. Obviously, it is best to have as few people who speak the same language in each discussion group as possible. Small discussion groups are best because: (1) students often feel more willing to talk among themselves in a small group than with a teacher in a large group; (2) the small discussion group often puts shy students more at ease; (3) the fewer people there are in the discussion group, the more English each group member must speak. The over-all goal of the small discussion group is to avoid the harrowing question-and-answer session that all too often constitutes discussion classes.

It is important that the teacher be flexible. One unit a day will tire even the most energetic students, as will a method of presentation that never varies. Because flexibility is so important, the following method of presentation is given merely as a suggestion, as a starting point to build upon and change.

Step-by-Step Guide for Classroom Use

A. *Class day before the unit will be used (can be done on the day the unit is used with more advanced classes)*

   1. Take 10–20 minutes to preview the unit with the class. Go over the Vocabulary section (and any other vocabulary in the unit that you think might pose a problem for students). Read the Read and Consider and Decide and Write sections aloud while the students read along silently. Make sure your students understand the problem.

   2. Assign the unit as homework. Ask students to read the unit again (except for the Extend section) and to write down their choices in the Decide and Write section.

B. *Class day the unit is used*

   1. (*10 minutes*) Preview the unit again. Ask the students if there were any ideas, words, and so on they did not understand. Try to relate the subject of the unit to the students' personal experience. (For example, for Unit 1 you can ask the students what questions they were asked when they first arrived in the United States.)

   2. Carefully divide the class into small discussion groups. Strive for heterogeneity.
      a. Vary the number of students in the groups. For Unit 1 you might divide the class into groups of four, for Unit 2 groups of five, for Unit 3 groups of two (as stated in the Preface, four to six is an ideal number but should not be followed always).
      b. Separate language groups as much as possible. Try not to have a discussion group composed of students who all speak the same language.
      c. Consider gender. Generally strive for male and female members in each group—but as an occasional variation you might try all female and all male groups.

      d. Be aware of any similarities that could produce homogeneity (which in a small discussion group values-clarification often translates into nondiscussion), such as age and religion.

      e. Most important, be sensitive to students' personalities. Try to spread gregarious or loquacious students throughout the groups as much as possible. Occasionally, put shy students and extroverted students into separate groups (this works better if the groups are not in the same room).

3. (*minimum 25 minutes*) Give the students a specific time in which to discuss the unit as a group. You might instruct them to start by reading aloud through each other's answers, then to work toward a group decision (the issue of how to proceed will normally work itself out among the members of the group). During these 25 (or more) minutes the teacher can:

      a. Move from group to group facilitating or stimulating discussion (I actually discourage this as much as possible because it places the teacher at the center of the discussion).

      b. Write grids or outlines on the board to be used in the next stage of comparing answers.

      c. Occupy herself or himself with other matters (if the discussions are going well—as a show of confidence in the students).

      d. Circulate around the class, listening to what is being said—making mental notes of points you might make in the next stage.

4. (*15–20 minutes*) (may occur on the next day if Step 3 lasts longer) Let the groups compare answers with each other as a class (can be done verbally or written on a blackboard). Ask students to describe how decisions were made—what other people in the group thought/think. This period should be lively with students/groups called upon to defend their positions/choices. (Be sure the students direct their comments to each other and not to you.)

5. (*5 minutes*) Go over the Extend section and assign it for homework.

C. Class day after main discussion.

Go over the Extend questions or activities.

U.S. Department of Justice
Immigration and Naturalization Service

FORM G-325A
BIOGRAPHIC INFORMATION

OMB No. 1115-0066
Approval expires 4-30-85

(Family name) (First name) (Middle name)	☐ MALE ☐ FEMALE	BIRTHDATE(Mo.-Day-Yr.)	NATIONALITY	FILE NUMBER A
ALL OTHER NAMES USED (Including names by previous marriages)	CITY AND COUNTRY OF BIRTH			SOCIAL SECURITY NO. (If any)

	FAMILY NAME	FIRST NAME	DATE, CITY AND COUNTRY OF BIRTH(If known)	CITY AND COUNTRY OF RESIDENCE.
FATHER				
MOTHER(Maiden name)				

HUSBAND(If none, so state) OR WIFE	FAMILY NAME (For wife, give maiden name)	FIRST NAME	BIRTHDATE	CITY & COUNTRY OF BIRTH	DATE OF MARRIAGE	PLACE OF MARRIAGE

FORMER HUSBANDS OR WIVES(if none, so state)

FAMILY NAME (For wife, give maiden name)	FIRST NAME	BIRTHDATE	DATE & PLACE OF MARRIAGE	DATE AND PLACE OF TERMINATION OF MARRIAGE

APPLICANT'S RESIDENCE LAST FIVE YEARS. LIST PRESENT ADDRESS FIRST.

STREET AND NUMBER	CITY	PROVINCE OR STATE	COUNTRY	FROM MONTH	YEAR	TO MONTH	YEAR
						PRESENT TIME	

APPLICANT'S LAST ADDRESS OUTSIDE THE UNITED STATES OF MORE THAN ONE YEAR

STREET AND NUMBER	CITY	PROVINCE OR STATE	COUNTRY	FROM MONTH	YEAR	TO MONTH	YEAR

APPLICANT'S EMPLOYMENT LAST FIVE YEARS. (IF NONE, SO STATE.) LIST PRESENT EMPLOYMENT FIRST

FULL NAME AND ADDRESS OF EMPLOYER	OCCUPATION(SPECIFY)	FROM MONTH	YEAR	TO MONTH	YEAR
				PRESENT TIME	

Show below last occupation abroad if not shown above. (Include all information requested above.)

THIS FORM IS SUBMITTED IN CONNECTION WITH APPLICATION FOR: ☐ NATURALIZATION ☐ STATUS AS PERMANENT RESIDENT ☐ OTHER (SPECIFY):	SIGNATURE OF APPLICANT	DATE
Are all copies legible? ☐ Yes	IF YOUR NATIVE ALPHABET IS IN OTHER THAN ROMAN LETTERS WRITE YOUR NAME IN YOUR NATIVE ALPHABET IN THIS SPACE	

PENALTIES: SEVERE PENALTIES ARE PROVIDED BY LAW FOR KNOWINGLY AND WILLFULLY FALSIFYING OR CONCEALING A MATERIAL FACT.

APPLICANT: BE SURE TO PUT YOUR NAME AND ALIEN REGISTRATION NUMBER IN THE BOX OUTLINED BY HEAVY BORDER BELOW.

COMPLETE THIS BOX (Family name)   (Given name)   (Middle name)   (Alien registration number)

How Will You Ask These Personal Questions?

Vocabulary

form a printed paper
immigration movement to a new country
over 3,000,000 more than 3,000,000
miscellaneous other, different

fill out to write down information
complete to finish
boss a person you work for
at least no less than

Read and Consider

The number of visitors to the United States increases each year. In 1950, about 100,000 foreign tourists, students and businesspersons came to the United States. But in 1990, over 3,000,000 foreign visitors came to America.

Every one of those foreign visitors filled out a short personal information form. This form gave the Department of Immigration information about each visitor.

You are new workers for the U.S. Department of Immigration. Your job is to interview tourists using the personal information form. Your boss wants you to practice making questions from the information in the boxes on the form.

Decide and Write

Read the form. In the spaces after the form, make questions to ask the people you will interview.

United States of America
Department of Immigration
Foreign Visitor Division

Form 3BF2z
Foreign Visitor Information Form

Personal Information:

Example: 1. Name: <u>What's your name?</u>

2. Country: _____

3. Height: _____

4. Weight: _____

5. Hair color: _____

6. Age: _____

7. Birthdate: _____

8. Reason for coming to the U.S.: _____

_____

9. Places you will visit: _____

10. Length of stay: _____

11. Mother's and father's names: _____

12. A. Marital Status: _____

　　　B. Spouse's name (if married): _____

13. Job: _____

14. Kind of Visa: _____

15. Address in your country: _____

_____

Discuss

Verbally compare your questions with those of your classmates in your discussion group. Is there more than one way to ask a question? When your group finishes, ask the questions to at least three of your classmates. Write down their answers. Then tell the class about one of the people you interviewed.

Extend

1. Should the immigration form ask for information about race, religion, and political views? Explain.

2. Should there be a limit on the number of people from one country that can visit the United States each year? For example, should the United States permit an unlimited number of Cubans or South Africans to visit each year?

3. Should the government of any country ask its visitors personal questions? Why or why not?

4. Ask one more person in your class the questions on your form. Write down their answers on your form. Then write a composition about your classmate (name, age, country, and so on).

Timbo's Dating Service: Who Dates Whom?

Vocabulary

for a change for a different experience

previous before now

blind date date in which the dating partners have never seen each other before

Read and Consider

You work for Timbo's Dating Service. Every day people come to your service in search of love. More specifically, some want to find a possible husband or wife.

Today you have 15 people (eight women, seven men). Your job is to put the couples together.

Women	*Men*

Woman 1: Sue Smith
Age: 33
Physical: 5′0″, 155 lbs
Previous marital experience: divorced, one child (4 years old)
Job: bank clerk ($22,000/year)
Hobbies: bicycling; running; going to football games
Statement: I want to marry a person who likes to go outside and do things.

Woman 2: Miriam Boesky
Age: 21
Physical: 5′4″, 99 lbs
Previous marital experience: none
Job: none
Hobbies: sitting in the sun; going to parties
Statement: I want to marry a rich, good-looking guy.

Woman 3: Martha Samuels
Age: 27
Physical: 6′2″, 180 lbs
Previous marital experience: none
Job: musician in symphony ($37,500)
Hobbies: reading; writing
Statement: I am looking for a family man who would be a good father. I want to have lots of children.

Woman 4: Elizabeth Frampton
Age: 26
Physical: 5′5″, 200 lbs
Previous marital experience: divorced (no children)
Job: electrical engineer ($32,500)
Hobbies: going to concerts; horseback riding
Statement: I am very romantic. I want a man to share love with.

Man 1: Sam Jones
Age: 32
Physical: 5′5″, 210 lbs
Previous marital experience: divorced (three children: 12, 10, 7)
Job: truck driver ($27,000)
Hobbies: watching TV; drinking beer
Statement: I want to meet a woman who has not been married before.

Man 2: Peter Wimsey
Age: 29
Physical: 6′1″, 160 lbs
Previous marital experience: none
Job: dancer
Hobbies: going to plays and concerts
Statement: I want a warm, cultured companion. I do not want an overweight woman. I don't want children.

Man 3: Joshua Zizov
Age: 38
Physical: 6′3″, 175 lbs
Previous marital experience: married three times (no children)
Job: banker ($250,000)
Hobbies: making money and spending it
Statement: I want a smart, good-looking woman.

Man 4: Frank Bissett
Age: 52
Physical: 5′10″, 170 lbs
Previous marital experience: divorced (five children: 28, 27, 24, 22, 21)
Job: airline pilot ($75,000)
Hobbies: woodworking
Statement: I want a woman that I can relax and be myself with.

Women	*Men*

Woman 5:   **"Charlie" Brinkley**
Age: 41
Physical: 5'7", 105 lbs
Previous marital experience: divorced two times (no children)
Job: model ($115,000)
Hobbies: fast cars; dancing
Statement: I just want to have fun. I don't want a man with children.

Woman 6:   **Mary Myers**
Age: 23
Physical: 5'3", 110 lbs
Previous marital experience: divorced (two children: 5, 6)
Job: student
Hobbies: going to movies; watching TV
Statement: Age and looks are not important to me. I just want to meet a nice guy for a change.

Woman 7:   **Jackie Kwan**
Age: 29
Physical: 5'9", 120 lbs
Previous marital experience: none
Job: karate teacher ($25,000)
Hobbies: motorcycling; playing baseball
Statement: I would like to meet an active man.

Woman 8:   **Racheline Johnson**
Age: 33
Physical: 4'11", 105 lbs
Previous marital experience: divorced (three children: 11, 6, 3)
Job: none
Hobbies: going for walks; playing with my children
Statement: I want to find a nice family man.

Man 5:   **Charles Meyer**
Age: 20
Physical: 6'1", 185 lbs
Previous marital experience: none
Job: graduate student (physical education) (no income)
Hobbies: all sports
Statement: Hey, I just want to have a good time.

May 6:   **Maynard Lacy**
Age: 35
Physical: 5'1", 150 lbs
Previous marital experience: divorced (one child: 18)
Job: salesman ($25,000)
Hobbies: walking; going to movies
Statement: I am ready to try anything!

Man 7:   **Robert Fisher**
Age: 26
Physical: 6'5", 200 lbs
Previous marital experience: none
Job: police officer ($30,000)
Hobbies: basketball
Statement: I don't want a serious relationship now.

Decide and Write (use last names only)

Couple 1: _____

Reason: _____

Couple 2: _____

Reason: _____

Couple 3: _____

Reason: _____

Couple 4: _____

Reason: _____

Couple 5: _____

Reason: _____

Couple 6: _____

Reason: _____

Couple 7: _____

Reason: _____

Discuss

Verbally compare your pairings with those of your classmates in your discussion group. Did they think about age, job, and interests carefully? Explain your opinions. Finally, the group needs to agree on its decisions. One person in the group should write down the group's decision.

Extend

1. What was the nicest date you ever had? (If you've never had one, imagine.)

2. Do you think it is good to date many people before a person marries? Explain.

3. What do you think about "blind dates"?

4. Should dates be arranged by the parents of the couple?

Making the Punishment Fit the Crime!

Vocabulary

jury   group that makes legal decisions

case   legal situation

manslaughter   accidental killing

death penalty   punishment by death

rape   forced sex

committed   did

promise   to say something will be done

prison   large jail for major criminals

assault   to attack someone, to hurt that person

unemployed   not having a job

suffer   to feel pain

Read and Consider

You are members of a jury in Portland, Oregon. Today, you will discuss the cases of six criminals. All six of the criminals said that they committed the crimes. You can punish a person with a warning, a fine, jail, or a combination of these, but Oregon does not have a death penalty.

The maximum punishments for the following crimes are:

Assault: five years   Rape: seven years

Breaking and entering: three years   Theft: three years

Drunk driving: six months   Manslaughter: four years

Murder: life imprisonment

Decide and Write

1. **Charles Mercer**, age 80, retired
   Crime: Murder
   Case Description: Mercer and his wife, Sara, had been married for 52 years. Sara got cancer in 1988 and was dying. She had been in the hospital for eight months and was kept alive by a respirator. On February 3, Charles Mercer went to the hospital and shot his wife. He says: "I loved her so much I couldn't watch her suffer anymore."

   Your Punishment: _____

   Reason: _____

2. **Ruth Tipton**, age 73, housewife, divorced (no children)
   Crimes: drunk driving; manslaughter
   Case Description: Mrs. Tipton is an alcoholic. She was in the hospital for a long time because of this. In the past ten years, police arrested Mrs. Tipton four times for drunk driving. On July 10, Mrs. Tipton was driving home from an afternoon party; she was drunk. She hit a 3-year-old girl on a tricycle. The girl died. Mrs. Tipton says: ''I'm so sorry; I promise to pay the little girl's parents some money every month. I will never drink again.''

   Your Punishment: _____

   Reason: _____

3. **George Raveling**, age 18, high school dropout
   Crime: theft (shoplifting)
   Case Description: On July 28, Raveling went to a grocery store with two of his friends. While there, he put 13 bars of candy in his pocket and tried to leave without paying. The manager caught him. He says: ''I'm really sorry. I didn't know I had to pay for the candy.''

   Your Punishment: _____

   Reason: _____

4. **Paul Jones**, age 35, unemployed, married (two children)
   Crimes: breaking and entering; theft
   Case Description: Mr. Smith lost his job at a wood factory two years ago. His wife also is unemployed. On the night of December 22, Mr. Smith stole two bicycles from the Peugeot Bicycle Shop. No one was in the store at the time of the robbery. Police caught him and found the bicycles the next day. Mr. Smith says: ''I only wanted to give my kids something for Christmas.''

   Your Punishment: _____

   Reason: _____

5. **Jimmy Jackson**, age 24, taxicab driver
   Crimes: assault; rape
   Case Description: On the evening of January 1, Mr. Williams and his girl-friend had a big fight. Later, on the way home, he went to a bar and got drunk. He saw two university girls (ages 18 and 19) alone in the bar, and he followed them out to their car at about 1:00 A.M. There, he beat them both, and he raped them. Mr. Williams says: ''The fight with my girlfriend and the alcohol made me crazy. I am sorry.''

   Your Punishment: _____

   Reason: _____

6. **Susan Smith**, age 43, secretary, widow (four children)
   Crime: murder
   Case Description: In the last seven years, Mrs. James has called the police eight times. Each time, she told police her husband was hitting her. In fact, she went to the hospital with serious injuries four times last year. On March 6, police received a call from Mrs. James's neighbor. They went to the James's house. They found Mrs. James with a gun in her hand. Mr. James was on the floor, dead. Mrs. James says: ''I'm not sorry I shot my husband. I thought he wanted to kill me.''

   Your Punishment: _____

   Reason: _____

Discuss

Verbally compare your punishments with those of your classmates in your discussion group. Listen carefully. Explain your opinions. Finally, the group needs to agree on its decisions. One person in the group should write down the group's decision.

Extend

1. Is it ever okay to steal?

2. When a soldier shoots an enemy soldier, is that murder? Write a definition of murder.

3. Will you call the police if you see a person speeding very fast in a car? you see a person stealing a book from a bookstore?

4. Should the death penalty ever be used? If no, why not? If yes, for what crimes?

Geneva: A New Beginning

Vocabulary

discuss   to talk about

industrialized   with many factories

developing   not industrialized

successful   having good results

weapon   anything used for fighting

debt   money owed

committee   a group with a special job

enemy   one that hates another

conference   a meeting to discuss a subject

gap   space between

Read and Consider

During 1988 and 1989, the world became more peaceful. World leaders began to solve such problems as Iran–Iraq, Angola, Cyprus, Kampuchea, and Afghanistan. Many successful discussions took place in Geneva, Switzerland.

   Now the world's leaders are going to have a larger conference to discuss more of the world's problems. You are members of the planning committee. You must decide the following:

1. Where will the leader from each country sit? (Friends or enemies should not sit beside each other.)

2. What will the leaders discuss?

Decide and Write

A. Leaders from the following countries will come. Write each country's name at a place around the conference table.

Iran	Sweden	Algeria
West Germany	India	Japan
Zimbabwe	Vietnam	Iraq
Israel	France	North Korea
Nigeria	South Africa	Mexico
Cuba	China	Central African Rep.
Egypt	South Korea	Brazil
Kampuchea	Pakistan	United Kingdom
Syria	Turkey	East Germany

Conference Table
Geneva

U.S.A.

U.S.S.R.

B. Rank these problems from 1 (most important) to 11 (least important):

_____ air and water pollution   _____ trade policies

_____ U.S.A./U.S.S.R.   _____ Arab-Israeli problem

_____ nuclear weapons   _____ AIDS

_____ debt of developing   _____ shortage of food
        countries

                                          _____ gap between rich and
_____ South Africa   poor people

_____ northern Ireland

C. Write down eight more important problems in the world (the leaders at the meeting will also discuss these problems):

1. _____

2. _____

3. _____

4. _____

5. _____

6. _____

7. _____

8. _____

Discuss

Verbally compare your decisions with those of your classmates in your discussion group. Listen carefully. Explain your opinions. Finally, the group needs to agree on its decisions. One person in the group should write down the group's decision.

Extend

1. What do you think is the world's biggest problem?

2. How can the United Nations stop countries such as the U.K., China, France, the U.S.A., and the U.S.S.R. from making nuclear weapons?

3. Imagine that all the world is one country and that you are the president. What is the first thing you would do?

4. Do you think that wars will ever stop? Explain.

Which Job Should I Try For?

Vocabulary

shift time of working
raise pay increase
environment surroundings
convalescent hospital hospital for
   senior citizens

EOE equal opportunity employer
wage salary
preferred wanted

Read and Consider

You are an unmarried, male, 22-year-old immigrant to the United States (Cleveland, Ohio). You were a taxicab driver in your country, and you came to the United States five months ago to get a better job. However, it is very difficult to find a good job because you don't have a university degree and your English is not good.

   You are studying English three times a week at night in an adult school near your apartment. However, life is expensive! You are spending about $1200 a month (for a very cheap apartment, cheap food, cheap clothes, and so on), and the $6000 you brought with you is almost gone.

   You must get a job this week (you just got your Green Card). The jobs on the next page are listed in the newspaper today.

Decide and Write

Study the following employment ads. Then rate the jobs from 1 = best for you, to 11 = worst for you.

CLEVELAND CLASSIFIED ADS/EMPLOYMENT WANTED

Full-time position. Day shift **laundry/housekeeping**. Contact Sandy Magill at Jones Health Care Convalescent Hospital, 715 Hyperion Way, Cleveland. 758-0553. EOE

GENERAL CLEANING/ MAINTENANCE, Monday–Friday: 3–4 Hours a day, $4.35/hour. Call 756-4242 or 758-2309

$350/Day! At home! Process phone orders for our products. People call you. Nationwide. Free details. 1-518-459-4047, Ext. B-9254

Waitresses/Waiters. If you are an energetic person with prior experience in food service, BON APPETITE RESTAURANT may have an excellent opportunity for you. We provide a complete training program and pleasant environment. Applicant must be at least 20 years old and available to work evening and morning shifts. Apply in person. Mon–Sun 7am–9pm, 400 Castle Court. EOE

DOMINOES PIZZA now hiring drivers. Must have own car + insurance (over 18). Min. wage + tips. 803 Russell Blvd. between 10am and 9 pm

WANT $8,422 PART TIME?
JOIN THE ARMY RESERVE with a needed skill and get $2000. Earn $1,382 a year for training. Get up to $5040 in GI benefits.
Call Sgt. Simon Bill
377-4662
Cleveland
BE ALL THAT YOU CAN BE!!!

GENERAL HELP
12 women or men to start immediately who are interested in changing their kind of work. $1320/month per agreement. Training provided. Setting up and showing appliances. No experience necessary. Call Morley: Thursday only between 8am and 5pm, 916-661-1007

Airlines now hiring. Flight attendants, travel agents, mechanics, customer service. Salaries to $105K. Entry-level positions. Call 916-758-0196. Ext K315

McDONALD'S of South Cleveland is now hiring. Full- and part-time shifts available anytime. Offering half-price meals, free uniforms, regular raises based on performance. Starting wage $4.75/hour. Apply any time in person. EOE

If you are big, friendly and not afraid of hard work, **THE NORTHSIDE BAR** is now hiring a few nighttime security positions. Apply in person: 337 Harrod St. NW, weekdays 1–3pm

Full-time position for quality assurance in busy Pathology Lab. Lab exp. preferred but not necessary. Mon–Fri 9–6, $5/hr. Call 422-3700 Ext 543. Deanna Reynes

Job 1: _____

   Reason: _____

   _____

   _____

Job 2: _____

   Reason: _____

   _____

   _____

Job 3: _____

   Reason: _____

   _____

   _____

Job 4: _____

   Reason: _____

   _____

   _____

Job 5: _____

   Reason: _____

   _____

   _____

Job 6: _____

   Reason: _____

_____

_____

Job 7: _____

   Reason: _____

_____

_____

Job 8: _____

   Reason: _____

_____

_____

Job 9: _____

   Reason: _____

_____

_____

Job 10: _____

   Reason: _____

_____

_____

Job 11: _____

   Reason: _____

_____

_____

Discuss

Verbally compare your choices with those of your classmates. When they chose the best jobs, did they look at all the facts? Are there any jobs that would be difficult for new immigrants? Support your opinions with examples. Agree as a group on one list.

Extend

1. Are there any jobs you would *not* do? Give examples.

2. Should a worker expect some benefits (such as health care, vacation time)? Explain.

3. Rate the following in importance when looking for a job (1 = most important, 6 = least important):

    _____ opportunity for promotion   _____ salary

    _____ benefits   _____ working conditions (boss, co-workers, situation)

    _____ working hours

    _____ using English language

4. Bring a copy of a local newspaper's classified ads to class and discuss with your class the jobs you find.

What Will They Look Like? What Will You Ask Them?

Vocabulary

beings   ''people''

Read and consider

The year is 2235. The Earth is receiving communications from space. Strange beings from another part of the universe are going to visit the Earth.

You will be in the group that meets the space beings. What do you think they will look like? What questions will you ask them?

Decide and Write

1. In the space below, draw a picture of one of the space beings. Fill in the description.

Height: _____

Weight: _____

Other Characteristics: _____

_____

2. What are 12 questions you want to ask them?

   1. _____

   2. _____

   3. _____

   4. _____

   5. _____

   6. _____

   7. _____

   8. _____

9. _____

10. _____

11. _____

12. _____

Discuss

Compare your drawing with the drawings of your classmates in your discussion group. Who used the most imagination? Explain your drawing. Finally, the group needs to agree on the 12 questions. One person in the group should write down the group's decision.

Extend

1. Do you think that space beings exist?

2. Would you like to go into space? Explain.

3. Do you think the space program is useful? Explain.

4. If space beings came to Earth, how would it change the Earth?

Our Student Association is Bankrupt!

Vocabulary

bankrupt   without money
project   activity

concert   musical performance

Read and Consider

The Association of University of California Students (ASUC) gives money to poor students, community groups, and university projects. But last year the Association gave out more money than it received. As a result, the ASUC is bankrupt.

In the past, the ASUC received money from the university. But this year the university has no extra money, so the ASUC will have to get its own.

You are members of the ASUC Board of Directors. You must think of projects to get money for the ASUC.

Decide and Write

A. **Concerts:** The university says you can use the recreation hall (16,000 seats) for five musical concerts. Choose five performers or groups to play for the concerts. *You must choose three performers or groups not on the following list.*

Possibilities

Whitney Houston
The New York Philharmonic
    Orchestra
Eric Clapton
Count Basie & Orchestra
Phil Collins
Vienna Boys Choir
Bobby McFerrin
U-2
Carlos Montoya
Billy Ocean
Stevie Wonder

INXS
Anita Baker
Michael Jackson
Julliard String Quartet
Luciano Pavarotti
Madonna
Bruce Springsteen
Barbara Streisand
Elton John
The Rolling Stones
Julio Iglesias
The Beach Boys

Name of Person or Group	*Kinds of Students That Will Come*
1. _____	_____
2. _____	_____
3. _____	_____
4. _____	_____
5. _____	_____

B. **Movies:** The university says you can show six movies in a large chemistry auditorium on campus. Any movie is available. You may choose movies not on the following list if you want.

Possibilities

Rocky XX
Gone With the Wind
Gandhi
Rambo X
The Godfather
Star Wars
Jaws
Emmanuelle
Rainman

Dirty Dancing
2001: A Space Odyssey
My Fair Lady
Top Gun
Casablanca
Singing In The Rain
Beverly Hills Cop II
The Terminator

Name of Movie	*Why Students Will Watch*
1.	
2.	
3.	
4.	
5.	
6.	

C. **Guest Lecturers:** You can invite five people to speak at the university this year. They can be actors, actresses, sports figures, politicians, authors, or people with any type of job. Here are some possibilities:

Possibilities

Jesse Jackson   George Bush
Mother Teresa   Martina Navratilova
Princess Diana   Tom Cruise
Prince Charles   Bill Cosby
Edward Kennedy   Alexander Solzhenitsyn

	Speaker	*Reason Why*
1.	_____	_____
2.	_____	_____
3.	_____	_____
4.	_____	_____
5.	_____	_____

Discuss

Verbally compare your decisions with those of your classmates in your discussion group. Listen carefully. Explain your opinions. Finally, the group needs to agree on its decisions. One person in the group should write down the group's decision.

Extend

Bring some music (record, tape) from your country to class (five-minute maximum). Play the music and explain it to your class. Show your class how to dance one of your country's dances.

Who Are the Best Citizens of Philadelphia?

Vocabulary

outstanding very good
citizen member of a country or
  city
nominate to suggest someone for
  an office or award

mayor head of a city
float to stay on top of water
beat up to hit a lot
seize to take by force

Read and Consider

Once a year the city of Philadelphia, Pennsylvania, chooses two outstanding citizens. These two citizens receive the ''Best Citizen of Philadelphia'' award. To receive this award a citizen first must help another person in the city. Then the citizen is nominated for the ''Best Citizen'' Award. Finally, the Philadelphia City Council looks at the nominations and chooses the two citizens to receive the award.

You are members of the Philadelphia City Council. This year you received 613 nominations. Last week you chose six finalists. Today you will choose the two winners.

Decide and Write

Citizen: Darrell Lombardo, age 11, elementary student. On the morning of April 2, Darrell was playing in Columbus Park. He saw a group of young boys. They were beating up an old man. First, Darrell threw rocks at the boys. Then he ran to a nearby policeman and told him. The policeman caught the boys and saved the old man.

Reasons to give (or not give) Lombardo the Award:

_____

_____

Order of importance: _____

Citizen: Sherry Handel, age 33, policewoman, unmarried. Ms. Handel is the leader of an anticocaine police group. This year her group arrested more than 50 drug dealers and seized more than 5000 pounds of cocaine. As a result, the number of cocaine users in Philadelphia decreased by 28% this year.

Reasons to give (or not give) Handel the Award:

_____

_____

Order of importance: _____

Citizen: Evelyn Hertz, age 91, social worker, widow (one child). Mrs. Hertz's husband was a very rich businessman. She always works hard to raise money for the poor people of Philadelphia. Also she tries to give the city important buildings. With her own money, she built the Hertz Opera Center (1976), the Hertz Free Medical Clinic (1985), and the Hertz Convention Center (1990).

Reasons to give (or not give) Hertz the Award:

_____

_____

Order of importance: _____

Citizen: Jun Sawada, age 65, accountant, married (five children). Mr. Sawada works for the city of Philadelphia. During the last year, he discovered his boss was stealing city money. His boss fired Mr. Sawada, but Sawada told the mayor. As a result, Mr. Sawada got his job back, his boss lost his job, and the citizens of Philadelphia saved $500,000.

Reasons to give (or not give) Sawada the Award:

_____

_____

Order of importance: _____

Citizen: Sofia Kolotrios, age 23, school bus driver, married (one child). On the rainy morning of October 29, Mrs. Kolotrios was driving her bus with 34 children to school. When the bus went down a hill, its brakes failed. With no way to stop the bus, Mrs. Kolotrios drove the bus into a telephone pole on the side of the street. This stopped the bus and saved the children. Mrs. Kolotrios died in the accident.

Reasons to give (or not give) Kolotrios the Award:

_____

_____

Order of importance: _____

Citizen: Louis Martinez, age 31, unemployed, unmarried. On the night of October 5, Mr. Martinez (homeless) was sleeping on Jackson Street. A fire started in one of the apartment buildings there. Mr. Martinez ran into the building and personally carried seven children to safety. Thirty people died in the fire.

Reasons to give (or not give) Martinez the Award:

_____

_____

Order of importance: _____

Discuss

Verbally compare your decisions with those of your classmates in your discussion group. Listen carefully. Explain your opinions. Finally, the group needs to agree on its decisions. One person in the group should write down the group's decision.

Extend

1. Should people receive awards because they help other people?

2. Would you die to save another person? to save your parents? your brothers and sisters? your aunts and uncles? your best friend? your teacher? Did you ever save another person? Explain.

3. Should rich people give their money to help poor people? If yes, how much? If no, why not?

4. Write a definition of a good citizen. Compare your definition with those of your classmates.

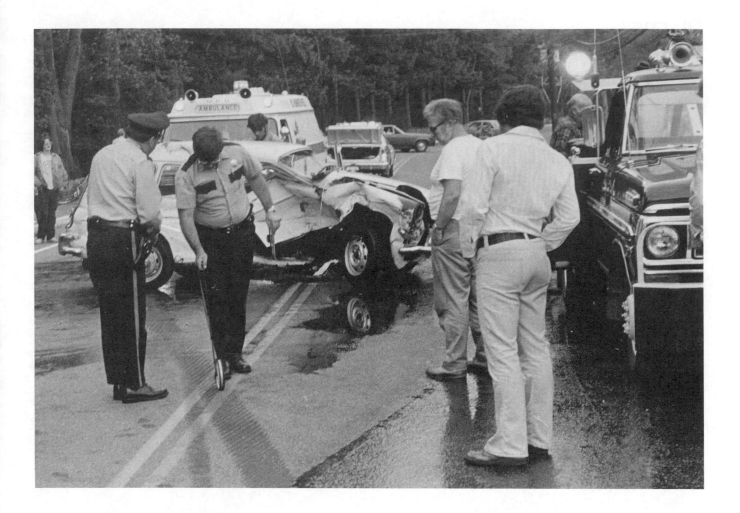

What Can We Do About Michigan's Drunk Drivers?

Vocabulary

drunk   too much alcohol in one's body

cause   to make happen

propose   to suggest

jail   a local prison

punishment   penalty for wrongdoing

breath   air that goes in and out of one's mouth or nose

speed   to go faster than the law allows

fine   money one pays for breaking the law

traffic   moving vehicles

Read and Consider

Drunk drivers cause over 50% of all traffic accidents in the United States, and they cause about 28,000 traffic deaths each year.

Michigan has more drunk-driving accidents than any other state. Last year, some people in Michigan started a group against drunk drivers. It is called MMADD (Michigan Mothers Against Drunk Driving).

You are members of the Michigan government. MMADD wants you to make stronger laws against drunk driving. Which laws will you change? How will you stop drunk driving?

Decide and Write

Possible New Limits and Laws

1. Most drunk-driving accidents happen in the 18–26 age group.

    Old Law: People must be 18 years old to drive in Michigan.
    Proposed New Law: People must be 21 years old to drive in Michigan.

    Which law is better? _____   Why? _____

2. Studies show that most drivers don't know how much alcohol can make them drunk.

    Old Law: (There is no law about driver's education courses.)
    Proposed New Law: Every new driver must take a driver's education course about the results of drinking alcohol.

    Which law is better? _____   Why? _____

3. Police say that most accidents with drunk drivers happen between 10 P.M. and 2 A.M.

   Old Law: (There is no law about when bars should close. They can stay open all night.)
   Proposed New Law: All Michigan bars must close at 12 midnight.

   Which law is better? _____ Why? _____

4. The police can give a breath test to find out who is drunk.

   Old Law: A person can refuse to take a breath test.
   Proposed New Law: A person cannot refuse to take a breath test.

   Which law is better? _____ Why? _____

New Fines and Punishments

Dangerous-Driving Act	Present Fine	New Fine	Present Jail	New Jail
1. Drunk driving—no accident happens; no other law is broken.				
First Time	$450	_____	3 days	_____
Second Time	$1000	_____	90 days	_____
2. Speeding while drunk				
1–20 mph over limit	$500	_____	3 days	_____
21+ mph over limit	$750	_____	90 days	_____
3. Causing an accident while drunk, no one dies	$1000	_____	6 mos.	_____
4. Causing an accident while drunk, a person dies	none	_____	10 yrs.	_____

Discuss

Verbally compare your decisions with those of your classmates in your discussion group. Listen carefully. Have you ever been in a car with a drunk driver? Support your opinions with examples and facts. Finally, the group needs to agree on its decisions. One person in the group should write down the group's decision.

Extend

1. If a drunk driver kills a person in a traffic accident, is the drunk driver guilty of murder? Is the person or business that gave him the alcohol guilty? Explain.

2. Would breath tests in bars help keep drunk people off the roads?

3. If you are at a party and you see someone drunk leave in a car, should you call the police?

4. Rate the following in order of danger (1 = most dangerous, 7 = least dangerous).

    _____ cocaine

    _____ alcohol

    _____ cigarettes

    _____ caffeine

    _____ tranquilizers

    _____ marijuana

    _____ heroin

Let's Put Some Pizzazz in the TV Schedule!

Vocabulary

audience people who see or watch an event

fire to remove from a job

garbage unused things or food we throw away

politics government activities

replace to take the place of

hire to give a job to someone

politician person in government

Read and Consider

The National Television Company (NTC) is losing its audience. Many years ago NTC was the best TV company in the United States; now it is the worst.

The owners of the network decided to end most of the old programs and add exciting new ones. They also fired the old programmers and hired you as the new programmers of NTC. You must make NTC Number One again.

Your research shows that most TV viewers in the United States are between 15 and 50 years of age, and that more women than men watch TV.

Decide and Write

Choose two of the following shows to put on the new NTC schedule:

New Show: *Gourmet Cooking* (educational)
This show will teach people how to cook unusual foods, such as coq au vin, baked Alaska, and truffles hollandaise. The program will also show viewers how to cook Chinese, Japanese, Brazilian, Greek, French, Israeli, and Italian food.

Reason to include (or not include) on the new schedule:

_____

_____

New Show: *Big Sur* (a nighttime soap opera)
This program shows the lives of a group of people living in Big Sur, California. Situations will show the problems and lives of the people in the program. In the first program, we will see a dentist who is in love with his wife, his dental assistant, and two of his female patients.

Reason to include (or not include) on the new schedule:

_____

_____

New Show: *Medical Team* (a drama)
This program will show daily lives of a hospital team in Miami, Florida. Situations will show special medical problems in the hospital. In the first show, doctors try to help a man with a bullet in his stomach and a woman with a bad heart.

Reason to include (or not include) on the new schedule:

_____

_____

New Show: *Kingdom* (a drama)

This program will show the lives of very rich and powerful members of an "oil" family in Riyadh, Saudi Arabia. We will see how they live and what they do to increase their money and power.

Reason to include (or not include) on the new schedule:

_____

_____

New Show: *Hollywood Garbagemen* (a comedy)

This program will show the funny life of two Hollywood garbage collectors. Situations will show the funny and unusual things inside the garbage cans of actors and actresses. In the first show, the garbagemen find $25,000 in the garbage can of a famous actress.

Reason to include (or not include) on the new schedule:

_____

_____

New Show: *Inside Art* (educational)

This show will teach people about art. The program will travel around the world and study famous paintings. On the first program, the show will go to Amsterdam's Rijksmuseum and study Rembrandt's "The Night Watch." During the first year, the program will show the paintings of Jan van Eyck, Tintoretto, Titian, Botticelli, El Greco, Velasquez, Manet, Chagall, and Kandinsky.

Reason to include (or not include) on the new schedule:

_____

_____

New Show: *The White House* (a comedy)

This program will show the funny side of politics in the United States. Situations will show that politicians are sometimes stupid and crazy. In the first show, a 70-year-old bad actor becomes president of the United States.

Reason to include (or not include) on the new schedule:

_____

_____

The two new programs you will include are:

_____   _____

Write a description of one *new* show you want writers to develop.

New Show: _____

Description: _____

_____

_____

Discuss

Verbally compare your decisions with those of your classmates in your discussion group. Listen carefully. Support your opinions with examples of good and bad TV shows you have seen. Finally, the group needs to agree on its decisions. One person in the group should write down the group's decision.

Extend

1. Do you think the government should control the programs on TV?

2. Does TV make society better or worse? List three positive effects and three negative effects of TV.

3. Do you think that TV will someday completely replace books? Why or why not?

4. Do you like to watch sports events, movies, plays, and concerts on TV, or do you like to watch them in person? Why?

Hearst Castle, built by William Randolph Hearst

Planning a House for the Richest Man in the City

Vocabulary

stream small river
style design
architecture way of building

property what a person owns
greenhouse glass room for plants

Read and Consider

You work for the Bailey and Curtis Company in Minneapolis, Minnesota. You design interesting new buildings and houses. Many people ask you to design new office buildings and new houses.

Today, the richest man in Minneapolis came to your office. He wanted your company to design his new house. He told you, "Cost is not important; I just want a big, warm, comfortable house for my wife, my four children, and me."

You must decide on the shape of the house, and the location (and shape) of the rooms inside the house.

The man wants the following things in his house:

Rooms	*Special Items*
6 bedrooms	1 swimming pool and patio
4 bathrooms	1 tennis court
8 (other) rooms (kitchen, livingrooms)	1 billiards room
1 big family playroom	1 exercise room
(lots of windows, glass doors, etc.)	1 greenhouse
	3 fireplaces

Decide and Write

Sketch your design for the house on this map.

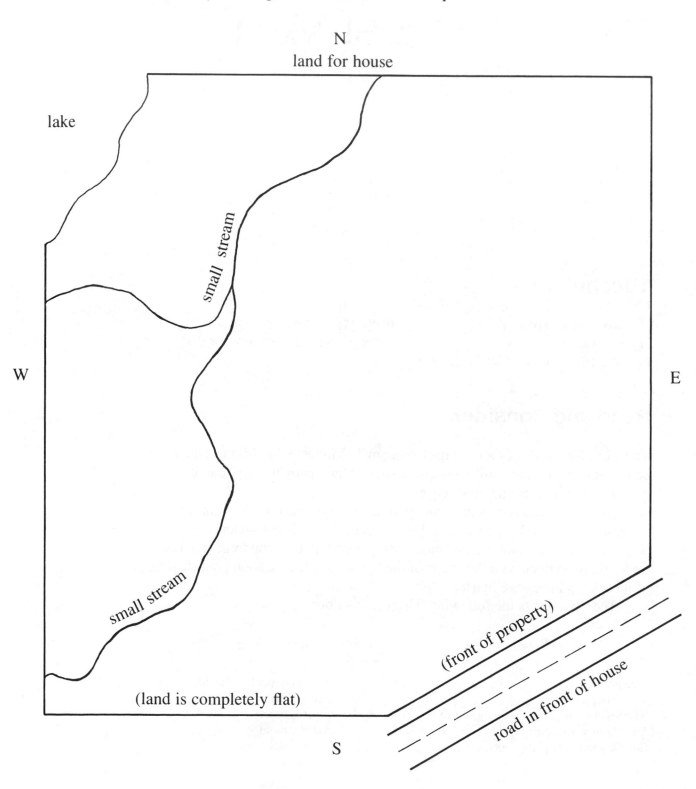

Discuss

Compare your design with those of your classmates. Choose the best one. Ask the ''winning'' designer to explain her or his design.

Extend

1. Bring to class pictures of houses and buildings in your country (or other countries). How is the architecture different from American architecture? Which style do you like best—modern? Japanese? Spanish? Arabic?

2. What are the advantages or disadvantages of having a house whose rooms have no doors?

3. What is the most unusual or interesting building you know? Describe it.

4. Describe your parents' house to your classmates.

How Will You Change the Olympics?

Vocabulary

participate   be a part of   **redesign**   change

Read and Consider

The Olympics are having many problems. In Munich (1972), terrorists killed Israeli athletes. In Moscow (1980), the United States refused to participate. In Los Angeles (1984), the U.S.S.R. and other Eastern European countries refused to participate. In Seoul (1988), Cuba and other countries refused to participate.

In addition to political problems, the Olympics are having problems with professionalism, drug use, and too many sports.

You are members of the International Olympic Committee (IOC). Your job is to redesign the Olympic Games.

Decide and Write

1. Instead of moving the games from one city to another, the IOC wants to choose one permanent summer city and one permanent winter city. Rank both of the following lists, from 1 (first choice) to 7 (last choice).

The choices for the summer Olympic city are:

_____ Montreal, Canada   _____ Sydney, Australia

_____ São Paolo, Brazil   _____ Amsterdam, Netherlands

_____ Algiers, Algeria   _____ Singapore, Singapore

_____ Istanbul, Turkey

The choices for the winter Olympic city are:

_____ Sapporo, Japan   _____ Zermatt, Switzerland

_____ Oslo, Norway   _____ Helsinki, Finland

_____ Edmonton, Canada   _____ Gothaarb, Greenland

_____ Reykjavik, Iceland

2. Every year the Olympics adds new sports. Now there are too many (over 237 events in 23 sports). The IOC wants to decrease the number of sports to only 25 individual events (same for men and women) and three team sports (same for men and women). A preliminary selection has already been made.

Choose 25 of the following. Put a check mark next to your choices.

Archery

_____ 10 m

_____ 100 m

Bicycling

_____ 20 km race

_____ 100 km race

Boxing

_____ 130 lb class

_____ 165 lb class

Canoeing

_____ 5 km

_____ 20 km

Diving

_____ 10 m platform

_____ 5 m springboard

Field

_____ shot put

_____ hammer throw

_____ discus

_____ javelin

_____ long jump

_____ pole vault

_____ high jump

_____ triple jump

_____ decathlon (ten events)

Gymnastics

_____ parallel bars

_____ vault

_____ sidehorse

_____ balance beam

_____ floor exercise

Rowing

———— 10 km

———— 50 km

Shooting

———— pistol (10 m)

———— rifle (100 m)

Swimming

———— 100 m freestyle

———— 100 m backstroke

———— 100 m breaststroke

———— 100 m butterfly

———— 400 m (medley: 100 m of each)

Horseback riding

———— steeplechase

Track

———— 100 m run

———— 400 m run

———— 5000 m run

———— 110 m hurdles

Weightlifting

———— 130 lb class

———— 165 lb class

———— 200 lb class

Wrestling

———— 130 lb class

———— 165 lb class

———— heavyweight

Choose three of the following team sports. Put a check mark next to your choices.

_____ baseball   _____ ping pong

_____ basketball   _____ tennis

_____ equestrian   _____ volleyball

_____ fencing   _____ yachting

Discuss

Verbally compare your decisions with those of your classmates in your discussion group. Listen carefully. Explain your opinions by talking about sports you have played or watched. Finally, the group needs to agree on its decisions. One person in the group should write down the group's decision.

Extend

1. Should professional athletes participate in the Olympics? Explain.

2. What do you think is the maximum number of athletes a country should have? (In Seoul [1988], the United States had 625 athletes; Brunei had one.)

3. Is it possible to separate sports from politics? If yes, how? If no, why not?

4. Should athletes be permitted to use drugs (such as steroids)? Why or why not?

5. Organize a competition in your class. It can be a sport or a game (such as chess).

Which Programs Will Get the Money?

Vocabulary

reduce   to make smaller, lower, or less

governor   the head of a state

request   an asking for

senior citizens   people over 65

legislature   group elected to make laws

condition   situation

ghetto   poor, run-down part of a city

conservation   saving from waste or loss

inflation   rise in prices

raise   more money in a salary

Read and Consider

State of California
Memo from the Governor's Office

17 July 1995

TO: California Office of Management and Budget (COMB)
FROM: Michael Holmquist, Governor
SUBJECT: $500,000 Surplus

The State of California has an extra $500,000 this year. I am going to use this money to help the citizens of our state. As you know, the state government reduced taxes last year. Many state programs stopped and others became smaller. For this and other reasons, my office received many requests for money.

Study the following requests. Make your suggestions. Remember, I want to return all $500,000 to the people.

Governor, State of California

Decide and Write

1. **Winters, California** (population (pop.) 23,000) Senior Citizens' Center
   Amount wanted: $87,000
   Reason: The Winters Senior Citizens' Center is very old, and it is in bad condition. We need to build a new one. There are over 5000 senior citizens in Winters.

   Amount of money to give: _____

   Why? _____

   _____

2. **Davis, California** (pop. 45,000) City Council
   Amount wanted: $75,000
   Reason: Our city always thinks about energy conservation. We want to build a new solar-heated swimming pool ($45,000) and a new train system ($30,000). The city will save $40,000 a year with these improvements.

   Amount of money to give: _____

   Why? _____

   _____

3. **State of California Legislature** (120 members)
   Amount wanted: $150,000
   Reason: We need a raise. Our salary of $40,000 a year is not enough to live on. We need a raise of $1250 a year because of inflation.

   Amount of money to give: _____

   Why? _____

   _____

4. **Los Angeles, California** (pop. 3,500,000) Public Works Department
   Amount wanted: $200,000
   Reason: Many people in the ghettoes of Los Angeles don't have jobs (35%). Most teenagers do not have jobs, and so robbery is increasing. We will use the money to give jobs to teenagers.

   Amount of money to give: _____

   Why? _____

   _____

5. **Carmel-by-the-Sea, California** (pop. 45,000) Beachfront Commission
   Amount wanted: $75,000
   Reason: In January, a big oil ship sank near our beautiful beach (the most beautiful in California). One hundred thousand gallons of oil filled the ocean and covered the beach. Thousands of birds and fish died. We need the money to clean up the mess.

   Amount of money to give: _____

   Why? _____

   _____

6. **San Luis Obispo, California** (pop. 85,000) Police Department
   Amount wanted: $75,000
   Reason: Crime is growing in our city. In 1986, five people were murdered; in 1988, 26 citizens were murdered. We need the money to hire two new policemen ($60,000) and to buy one new police car ($15,000).

   Amount of money to give: _____

   Why? _____

   _____

7. **San Francisco, California** (pop. 750,000) Health Department
   Amount wanted: $500,000
   Reason: San Francisco has the largest population of AIDS patients in the United States. Between 1987 and 1989, over 3000 San Franciscans died because of AIDS. We need the money to help stop the epidemic.

   Amount of money to give: _____

   Why? _____

   _____

Discuss

Verbally compare your decisions with those of your classmates in your discussion group. Listen carefully so you can report on what the people in your group think. Support your opinions. Finally, the group needs to agree on its decisions. One person in the group should write down the group's decisions.

Extend

1. What are the three most important jobs of a state government?

2. Should a government give jobs to people?

3. Is it better to have a large or a small national government? Why, or why not?

4. What is the best way for a government to fight crime?

Divorce! Who Gets What?

Vocabulary

divorce   separation by law
boring   uninteresting

alimony   support money

Read and Consider

Bill and Susan Gordon were married in West Virginia in 1976. For ten years they were very happy; they had a boy in 1979, and a little girl in 1983. In 1986 the Gordons moved to Connecticut, and they started to have problems with each other. Now they want to get a divorce.

You are members of a family court in Bridgeport, Connecticut. Study each story carefully, then decide who gets what.

Bill Gordon, 42, civil engineer ($40,000 a year)
Bill's Statement to the Court: "Susan is a good mother and a good person; in fact, I don't want a divorce, but I can't stop her. At home, both Susan and I take care of the children, and I do 50% of the cooking. I know our lives are not very exciting; we only go to a restaurant or movie once a week. But I love my children more than anything else in the world. After the divorce, I want: *the children 75% of the time, 50% of the furniture and property, one car, and the house* (because she is leaving me). *I don't want to pay her any alimony."*

Susan Gordon, 40, accountant ($35,000 a year)

Susan's Statement to the Court: "Bill is a great father; in fact, he always spends more time with the children than he spends with me. But after the kids are in bed, he always goes out to drink and play cards with the guys. Our life is very boring; we never do anything exciting. I still like him, but I just can't live with him anymore. I love my children very much, but I also want to be happy myself. After the divorce, I want: *the children 75% of the time, 50% of the furniture and property, one car, and the house* (because he is the reason for the divorce). *I want $15,000 a year in alimony.*"

Decide and Write

1. The children will be with:

    Susan _____% of the time; Bill _____% of the time.

    Reason: _____

    _____

2. *(Non-Furniture Property)*	*Bill's Property*	*Susan's Property*
A BMW 320i	_____	_____
A Chevrolet station wagon	_____	_____
A 24-inch RCA TV	_____	_____
A stereo system	_____	_____
A washer and dryer	_____	_____
A microwave oven	_____	_____
A hot tub	_____	_____

3. The house has four bedrooms, two bathrooms, and a swimming pool. Its value is $175,000.

   Who receives the house? _____

   Who must move out? _____

   Reason: _____

   _____

4. The Gordons have a $22,500 savings account.

   How much money will Susan get? _____

   How much money will Bill get? _____

   Reason: _____

   _____

5 Alimony: How much money will Bill pay Susan every year (until she

   remarries)? _____

   Why? _____

   _____

Opinion of the Court. In the space below, write five sentences about Bill, Susan, and the divorce.

_____

_____

_____

_____

_____

_____

_____

Discuss

Verbally compare your decisions with those of your classmates in your discussion group. Listen carefully. Explain your opinions. Do you know a divorced couple? Finally, the group needs to agree on its decisions. One person in the group should write down the group's decision.

Extend

1. The number of divorces is increasing. Give two reasons for this.

2. How is divorce good or bad for children?

3. When is divorce a good idea?

4. Sometimes a man and a woman live together before they get married. Does this help a marriage? Does it help to reduce the number of divorces?

Bishop Desmond Tutu, winner of the 1984 Nobel Peace Prize

Who Deserves the Nobel Peace Prize?

Vocabulary

contribution   what one gives to others

prize   award

treaty   written agreement between countries

majority   more than half of the people

march   a public walk

human rights   important freedoms for people

establish   make

Read and Consider

Every year the Nobel Prize Committee in Stockholm, Sweden, gives the Nobel Peace Prize to someone.* It is one of the highest awards a person can receive. A person receives the award for:

a. *A special contribution to peace.* For example, Henry Kissinger and Le Duc Tho received the 1973 Peace Prize because they ended the Vietnam War.

b. *A lifetime of contributions to peace.* For example, Dag Hammarskjold received the 1961 Peace Prize for his many contributions to peace as Secretary-General of the United Nations.

You are a member of the 1994 Nobel Peace Prize Committee. Choose the winner for the year.

Decide and Write

Nominee 1: **Henrick Von Damm**, South African Foreign Minister

Contribution to Peace: For many years, an all-white government ruled South Africa. Blacks fought against whites; there was a war there last year. Mr. Von Damm wrote a treaty to end the war. The black majority will now control the South African government.

Reason to give (or not give) Von Damm the prize: _____

_____

---

*It is possible for no one to receive the award. For example, no one received the Peace Prize in 1940–1943, 1948, 1955, 1966, 1967, and 1972.

It is possible for a *group* to receive the award. In 1954, the United Nations Office of Refugees received the Prize; in 1963, the International Red Cross won the award.

Nominee 2: **Bernadette Ross and Brendan Moriarity**, Irish Activists

Contribution to Peace: In the past, Ross and Moriarity had seven ''Save the Children'' marches in the streets of Dublin, Ireland. They also tried many other ways to stop the fighting between Catholics and Protestants in northern Ireland. During the 1993 march, a bomb killed Ross and Moriarity.

Reason to give (or not give) Ross and Moriarity the prize: _____

Nominee 3: **Mikhail Gorbachev**, First Secretary, U.S.S.R.

Contribution to Peace: Gorbachev helped to decrease nuclear weapons in Eastern Europe (1986). In 1987 he signed a treaty with Ronald Reagan to reduce the number of missiles in the U.S.S.R. and the U.S.A. In 1988 he started to take Soviet soldiers out of Afghanistan. In 1993, Gorbachev signed a peace treaty between the U.S.S.R. and China.

Reason to give (or not give) Gorbachev the prize: _____

Nominee 4: **Hosni Mohammed** (Palestinian representative) **and Benyamin Basset** (Israeli ambassador)

Contribution to Peace: In 1993, Mohammed and Basset wrote a peace treaty between Palestinians and Israelis. After 43 years, the Palestinians finally recognized Israel. Israel agreed to establish a Palestinian state in parts of the West Bank and Gaza.

Reason to give (or not give) Mohammed and Basset the prize: _____

Nominee 5: **UNICEF**, The United Nations' International Children's Emergency Fund

Contribution to Peace: UNICEF gives over $25 million a year to feed hungry children around the world. For example, in 1981 UNICEF sent food to save over 500,000 children in Ethiopia and Somalia. Last year UNICEF opened new offices in the Sudan and Bombay, India, to help hungry children there.

Reason to give (or not give) UNICEF the prize: _____

_____

The Winner of the 1994 Nobel Peace Prize is: _____

_____

(In case the winner does not accept), the second choice is:

_____

The main reasons we chose the winner (or did not choose a winner) are:

_____

_____

_____

_____

_____

Discuss

Verbally compare your decisions with those of your classmates in your discussion group. Listen carefully. Support your opinions with examples and facts. Finally, the group needs to agree on its decisions. One person in the group should write down the group's decision.

Extend

Find a new or old newspaper or magazine today that gives national and international news. Try to find an article that tells about someone who is working for peace. Bring the article (or a copy of it) to class. Write a short paragraph about the article and share it with your class.

Opening a New Restaurant

Vocabulary

terrible very bad
awful very bad

service way of giving food
customer a person who buys

Read and Consider

You live in Pitsville, Nevada. Your town does not have any good places to eat. The restaurants are bad. The pizza places are terrible. The chicken place is awful, and the hamburger places serve the worst hamburgers in the world! Residents of Pitsville must travel 40 miles to another city to find good food to eat.

At present there are six pizza parlors, three hamburger places, four sandwich shops, two delicatessens, one fried chicken store, one Mexican restaurant, one Greek restaurant, one Italian restaurant, one Chinese restaurant, and one French restaurant.

It is time to change the situation. You and your friends are going to open a new "international" restaurant. You want to do three things:

a. Serve good food at a fair price.

b. Give good service to your customers.

c. Make money for yourself.

Decide and Write

1. What time of the day will you open? _____
   close? _____

2. How many seats will be in the restaurant? _____

3. Describe generally the inside and the outside of the restaurant (color, style,

   and so on): _____

   _____

   _____

4. Make a sign to put on the outside of the building:

The Dinner Menu of the _____ restaurant

Soups and Salads

1. (dish name) _____ (cost) _____

   (description) _____

2. Chef's Greek salad _____ $2.50 _____

   fresh lettuce, cucumber, oils _____

3. _____   _____

_____

4. _____   _____

_____

Breads

1. _____   _____

2. _____   _____

Main Dishes

1. _____   _____

_____

2. _____   _____

_____

3. _____   _____

_____

4. _____   _____

_____

5. _____   _____

_____

Desserts

1. _____ _____

   _____

2. _____ _____

   _____

3. _____ _____

   _____

4. _____ _____

   _____

5. _____ _____

   _____

6. _____ _____

   _____

Beverages

1. Cafe au Chocolat (French) _____ $1.75 ___

2. _____ _____

3. _____ _____

4. _____ _____

5. _____ _____

6. _____ _____

7. _____ _____

8. _____ _____

Discuss

Verbally compare your decisions with those of your classmates in your discussion group. Listen carefully. Explain your opinions. Describe good restaurants at which you've eaten. Finally, the group needs to agree on its decisions. One person in the group should write down the group's decision.

Extend

1. Do you think the restaurant business is an easy business? Why, or why not?

2. What is the best restaurant you know? Why?

3. Do you want to own a small business and make $20,000 a year, or work for a large business and make $90,000 a year?

4. What are the most important things to think about when you choose a job?

   If possible, bring a food from your country and share it with your class. Write down the recipe and give it to your classmates. Explain to them how to make the dish.

How Can We Solve Our Problems?

Vocabulary

temporary not permanent
expired stopped
landlord owner of apartment
    building

afford have enough money

Read and Consider

You are a middle-aged foreign couple living in the United States. You came here to Milwaukee, Wisconsin, one year ago to escape from political problems in your country. You (the husband) have a permanent visa to stay in the United States, but you (the wife) only have a temporary visa, which expired last month. You (the wife) have applied for a permanent visa, but you have not received it yet. You (the wife) are now in the United States illegally.

During the last year, both of you have worked in part-time jobs. You got these jobs because of the agency that was sponsoring you (the agency stopped sponsoring you two months ago). At first, life was exciting; but now you are beginning to have many problems. How can you solve them?

Decide and Write

Problem 1: **Your (the wife's) visa**
You are now in the United States illegally, because your visa has expired. The Immigration and Naturalization Service (INS) says it will take at least five months to process your application for a new visa. You are very afraid that INS will send you back to your country. What can you do?

Recommendation: _____

_____

_____

Problem 2: **Poor condition of the apartment**
At first, your apartment looked very good. Now you have problems with the toilet in the bathroom, the heater throughout the apartment, and the refrigerator (which came with the apartment). The manager of the apartments says that these are your problems. You really like the apartment's location, and you don't want to move. What can you do?

Recommendation: _____

_____

_____

Problem 3: **Rent**
The landlord has been increasing your rent every two months. Six months ago your rent was $495 a month; now it is $645 a month. What can you do?

Recommendation: _____

_____

_____

Problem 4: **No health insurance**
You cannot afford private health insurance, and neither of you gets health insurance with your jobs. You are getting older, and you are very worried about what will happen if you get sick. What can you do?

Recommendation: _____

_____

_____

Problem 5: **Homesickness**
You are happy you came to the United States, but you miss your country very much. You have little opportunity to talk to your family and friends back there. Americans don't seem very friendly to you, and sometimes the whole situation makes you depressed.

Recommendation: _____

_____

_____

Discuss

Verbally compare your decisions with those of your classmates in your discussion group. Listen carefully; think of your own experiences. Have you ever had the same problems as the couple in the problem? Have you ever felt the same way? Explain your opinions. Finally, the group needs to agree on its recommendations. One person in the group should write down the group's decision.

Extend

1. Is it more difficult to immigrate to a country when you are young, middle-aged, or old? Explain.

2. In general, do you find it easy or difficult to solve problems in the United States? Explain with personal examples.

3. What is your opinion of Americans? Are they friendly? cold? happy? lazy? Explain with examples.

4. Write a composition about the biggest problem (or problems) you have had in the United States. (If you have never been to the United States, what is the biggest problem you think you would have?)

Where Are We Going to Build the New Airport?

Vocabulary

possible   that can be

expert   a person who knows a lot about a subject

population   number of people in a city, country, and so on

predict   to tell what will happen in the future

park   public land (usually beautiful)

propose   to suggest

Read and Consider

Davisville, Missouri, is a rapidly growing city. In 1960, 5000 people lived in Davisville; in 1980, 10,000 people lived there; now over 40,000 residents live in Davisville. Population experts predict a 100% rise in population in the next ten years.

Davisville needs an airport. The nearest airport is in Kansas City, 225 miles away. Many visitors come to Davisville to speak and study at the university.

You are the Davis County Planning Commission. Today you are studying a report about the new airport. There are five possible places to build it. You must choose one.

Decide and Write

Study the following map; then make your decisions.

Map of Davis County

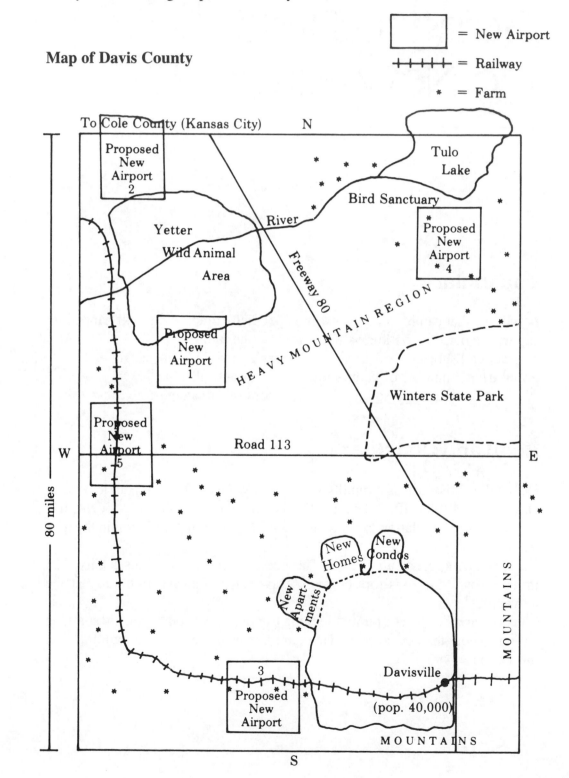

Proposed Airport 1: Thirty miles from Davisville

Advantages: _____

_____

_____

Disadvantages: <u>Hard to build an airport in mountains</u> _____

_____

_____

Proposed Airport 2: Seventy miles from Davisville

Advantages: <u>Cole County will pay half</u> _____

_____

_____

Disadvantages: _____

_____

_____

Proposed Airport 3: Five miles from Davisville

Advantages: _____

_____

_____

Disadvantages: <u>Jets must land and take off near many houses</u> _

_____

Proposed Airport 4: Thirty-five miles from Davisville

Advantages: <u>Only seven miles from big highway</u>

_____

_____

Disadvantages: _____

_____

_____

Proposed Airport 5: Thirty miles from Davisville

Advantages: _____

_____

_____

Disadvantages: <u>High cost: must move road 113 and railroad</u>

_____

_____

We want Proposed Airport #_____

Reasons: _____

_____

_____

_____

2nd choice: _____   4th choice: _____

3rd choice: _____   5th choice: _____

Discuss

Verbally compare your decisions with those of your classmates in your discussion group. Listen carefully so you can report what other people in your group think. Explain your opinions. Finally, the group needs to agree on its decisions. One person in the group should write down the group's decision.

Extend

Draw a map of your home town or home city. In general, do you think the town was well planned or poorly planned? Describe it to your class.

A Traveler's Guide

Vocabulary

guide   person or book that gives directions

Read and Consider

You work for the Touristo Book Company in Bangor, Maine. Your most important job is to write books for tourists in the United States. Right now, there is not a good, *small* book to help foreign tourists with English vocabulary, sentences, and questions.

Your editor wants you to write a good, short guide to English. He wants you to write only the most important things in English for foreign visitors.

Decide and Write

A. Write 15 important questions for a foreign visitor to know:

1. (Example) How much does it cost? _____

2. _____

3. _____

4. _____

5. _____

6. _____

7. _____

8. _____

9. _____

10. _____

11. _____

12. _____

13. _____

14. _____

15. <u>(Example) Where is the restroom, please?</u>

B. What are 30 important vocabulary words for the visitor?

<u>restaurant</u>   _____   _____

_____   _____   _____

_____   _____   _____

_____   _____   _____

_____   _____   _____

_____   _____   _____

_____   _____   _____

_____   _____   _____

_____   _____   <u>highway</u>

C. What are 15 important sentences for visitors to know?

1. Thank you very much for your help. _____

2. _____

3. _____

4. _____

5. _____

6. _____

7. _____

8. _____

9. _____

10. _____

11. _____

12. _____

13. _____

14. _____

15. _____

D. List ten foods or drinks.

water _____   _____

_____   _____

_____   _____

_____   _____

_____   bread _____

E. List 15 other language items, such as questions or expressions (you choose).

_____   _____   _____

_____   _____   _____

_____   _____   _____

_____   _____   _____

_____   _____   _____

F. Write five important customs for the tourist to know.

1. _____

2. _____

3. _____

4. _____

5. _____

G. Write five important facts to know about the United States.

1. Public transportation is not good. _____

2. _____

3. _____

4. _____

5. _____

Discuss

Verbally compare your decisions with those of your classmates in your discussion group. Listen carefully. Explain your opinions. What were the first English words, sentences, or questions you learned? Finally, the group needs to agree on its decisions. One person in the group should write down the group's decision.

Extend

1. Do you think that most Americans are friendly or cold?

2. What do you like the most about American society? What do you like the least?

3. Do you like English as a language? Is your language better?

4. Write a paragraph about three unusual things that Americans do.

Terrorist Attack: What Action Do We Take?

Vocabulary

release   to let go
policy   group of ideas for a
government, business, and
so on

blackmail   illegal payment to keep
information secret
negotiate   to discuss in order to
reach an agreement

Read and Consider

8:00 A.M., Wednesday, May 1
The president of the United States received the following telegram:

> We are the People's Liberation Army (PLA). At 3:00 a.m. this morning,
> we entered the Statue of Liberty in New York City. We have a nuclear
> bomb with us. The bomb will explode at 12:00 p.m. (noon) today, May 1.
> We will not explode the bomb if:
>
> (1) You release all 126 members of the PLA in U.S. prisons, and
> (2) You deliver $500,000,000 to us by noon.
>
> We will call the White House at 11:00 a.m. this morning to find out your
> answer. Remember, 15,000,000 New Yorkers will die if you say no!

The People's Liberation Army has a long history of terrorist attacks. Last year, they hijacked a plane, and wanted $1 million. The president refused to give them the money. The PLA blew up the plane (245 passengers and ten PLA members died). The FBI says that terrorists are in the Statue.

You are the National Security Council; the president wants you to make the decision. The president's policy is: "The United States will never give blackmail to terrorists."

Decide and Write

Choose a plan of action. Order these from 1 = best plan to 8 = worst plan.

Choice A. Do not tell the public. Do nothing. Hope the bomb threat is not real.

Order: _____

Advantage: _____

Disadvantage: _____

Choice B. Do not tell the public. Tell the FBI to go into the Statue and try to get the bomb.

Order: _____

Advantage: _____

Disadvantage: _____

Choice C. Do not tell the public. Release the prisoners and give the terrorists the money.

Order: _____

Advantage: _____

Disadvantage: _____

Choice D. Tell the public. Tell the FBI to attack the Statue after you try to get everyone out of the city.

Order: _____

Advantage: _____

Disadvantage: _____

Choice E. Do not tell the public. Tell the FBI about the situation, but do not do anything right away. Try to negotiate when the PLA calls at 11:00 A.M.

Order: _____

Advantage: _____

Disadvantage: _____

Choice F. Tell the public. Get everyone out of the city. Release the prisoners. Give the terrorists the money.

Order: _____

Advantage: _____

Disadvantage: _____

Choice G. Do not tell the public. Contact the Secretary-General of the United Nations. Ask him to negotiate.

Order: _____

Advantage: _____

Disadvantage: _____

Choice H. (Make your own plan.) _____

_____

_____ Order: _____

Advantage: _____

Disadvantage: _____

Discuss

Verbally compare your decisions with those of your classmates in your discussion group. Listen carefully. Explain your opinions. Has there been terrorism in your country? Finally, the group needs to agree on its decisions. One person in the group should write down the group's decision.

Extend

1. Write two definitions:

    a. A terrorist is a person who _____

    _____

    b. A freedom fighter is a person who _____

    _____

2. The president's policy is: "Never give blackmail to terrorists." Is this a good policy?

3. World terrorism is increasing. Why? Would you ever become a terrorist? Explain.

Design a U.S. Travel Brochure

Vocabulary

decrease   to go down in number or amount

department   a separate part of a government or business

partial   not complete

wonderful   excellent

brochure   papers with information

Read and Consider

Millions of tourists visit the United States every year. Some of these tourists only visit one place, such as Disneyland; other tourists try to visit many places in the United States.

Last year, the number of tourists to the United States decreased. This was very bad for the American tourist business. The government wants to increase the number of tourists in the future.

The government is going to advertise about great places to visit in the United States. The government wants you—workers in the U.S. Department of Commerce—to design a good travel brochure to bring tourists to the United States.

On the following page is a *partial* list of great places to visit.

Great U.S. Cities, and Places to See in Each City

Atlanta, Georgia: Peachtree Street, Underground Atlanta

Boston, Massachusetts: Bunker Hill, Boston Harbor

Charleston, South Carolina: Battery, Hilton Head

Chicago, Illinois: Sears Tower, Merchandise Mart

Denver, Colorado: U.S. Mint, Winter Park

Honolulu, Hawaii: Pearl Harbor, Waikiki Beach

Las Vegas, Nevada: Gambling casinos, Hoover Dam

Los Angeles, California: Disneyland, Hollywood, Beverly Hills

New Orleans, Louisiana: French Quarter, Bourbon Street

New York, New York: United Nations, Fifth Avenue, Statue of Liberty

Orlando, Florida: Disneyworld, Epcot Center

Philadelphia, Pennsylvania: Independence Park, Liberty Bell

St. Louis, Missouri: Gateway Arch, Mississippi River

Salt Lake City, Utah: Great Salt Lake, Mormon Temple

San Diego, California: San Diego Zoo, Tijuana

San Francisco, California: Fisherman's Wharf, Chinatown, Golden Gate Bridge

Santa Fe, New Mexico: Los Alamos, Navajo Museum, Taos

Seattle, Washington: Space Needle, Vancouver

Washington, D.C.:   White House, Jefferson-Lincoln-Washington Memorials, Smithsonian

Great Geographical Places

Alaskan National Parks

Badlands, South Dakota

Carlsbad Caverns, New Mexico

Everglades National Park, Florida

Glacier National Park, Montana

Grand Canyon, Arizona

Grant Teton National Park, Wyoming

Niagara Falls, New York

Okefenokee Swamp, Georgia

Rocky Mountains, Colorado

Volcano National Park, Hawaii

Yellowstone National Park,
    Wyoming-Montana

Yosemite National Park, California

Zion National Park, Utah

Great Events to See

Cheyenne Rodeo: Cheyenne,
    Wyoming

Indianapolis 500:   Indianapolis,
    Indiana

Kentucky Derby: Louisville,
    Kentucky

Macy's Thanksgiving Day Parade:
    New York City

Mardi Gras: New Orleans

Master's Golf Tournament:
    Augusta, Georgia

Rose Bowl Parade: Pasadena,
    California

Other Great Points of Interest

Cape Canaveral: Florida

Napa Valley vineyards: Napa,
    California

Shenandoah Valley, Virginia

Snow-skiing in Vermont and Idaho

Wheat and cornfields of Iowa and
    Nebraska

Decide and Write

Page 1

THIS IS YOUR YEAR TO SEE
THE U.S.A.!

Picture of _____
(Choose the most famous or beautiful place in the U.S. or in your city.)

YOU CAN FIND EVERYTHING!
in the United States!

Wonderful Cities (or Places Inside Your city)!

_____ (city)

_____ (1 sight)

_____ (1 sight)

Picture
of
_____

Picture
of
_____

_____ (city)

_____ (1 sight)

_____ (1 sight)

_____ (city)

_____ (1 sight)

_____ (1 sight)

Picture
of
_____

_____ (city)

_____ (1 sight)

_____ (1 sight)

Picture
of
_____

_____ (city)

_____ (1 sight)

_____ (1 sight)

Picture
of
_____

Page 2

WONDERFUL GEOGRAPHY (or PUBLIC PARKS/AREAS)

Picture of
_____

Picture of
_____

Picture of
_____

And!

(place) _____

_____

_____

_____

- -

GREAT EVENTS TO SEE!!!

Picture of
_____

Picture of
_____

Picture of
_____

Design this third page of the brochure yourselves. There must be six small pictures and one big picture on the page. Also write four sentences about the United States (or your city) at the top or bottom of the page.

Page 3

Discuss

Compare your brochure with those of your classmates in your discussion group. Listen carefully. Explain your opinions using examples from your travel or reading experience. Finally, the group needs to agree on its decisions. One person in the group should write down the group's decision.

Extend

Choose the three best places to visit in your country or city. Prepare a three-to-five-minute talk about them for your class. Bring pictures or slides, if possible. Tell your classmates about the places.

Leonardo da Vinci, Mona Lisa, *Louvre, Paris*

Editing and Writing a Newspaper

Vocabulary

editor   head of a newspaper
elect   to choose by voting
invade   to enter by force
income tax   money for the government from a salary
cure   a medicine that makes one well

accident   a sudden happening that may hurt a person
solar   from the sun
international   with many countries
design   plan
invent   make something new (like an airplane or a telephone)

Read and Consider

You are the editors of the *Chicago Times* newspaper. Every day you must make hundreds of decisions about stories to put in the newspaper. On many days, there is a small amount of news and your decisions are easy. But on other days, there is a lot of news and your decisions are difficult.

Today is a very unusual day! There are many exciting national and international stories. Which stories will be on pages 1, 2, and 3?

Decide and Write

Here are the headlines. The stories all happened yesterday afternoon, evening, and early this morning:

Fidel Castro Dies!

Scientist Finds Cure for Liver Cancer!

Dan Williams Elected Mayor of Chicago!

Russian Soldiers Invade China!

Four Feet of Snow in Los Angeles!

Peace in Israel!

U.S. Congress Stops Income Tax!

Thieves Steal Mona Lisa from Louvre!

Italy Wins World Cup!

Nuclear Accident in New York!

Plane Crash Kills 337 People!

OPEC Raises Prices 25%!

Thieves Rob Four Banks in Chicago!

Scientist Invents Solar-Powered Jet!

Iran and Iraq Fight Again!

Scientists Find Cure for AIDS!

A. Fill in a headline beside each number:

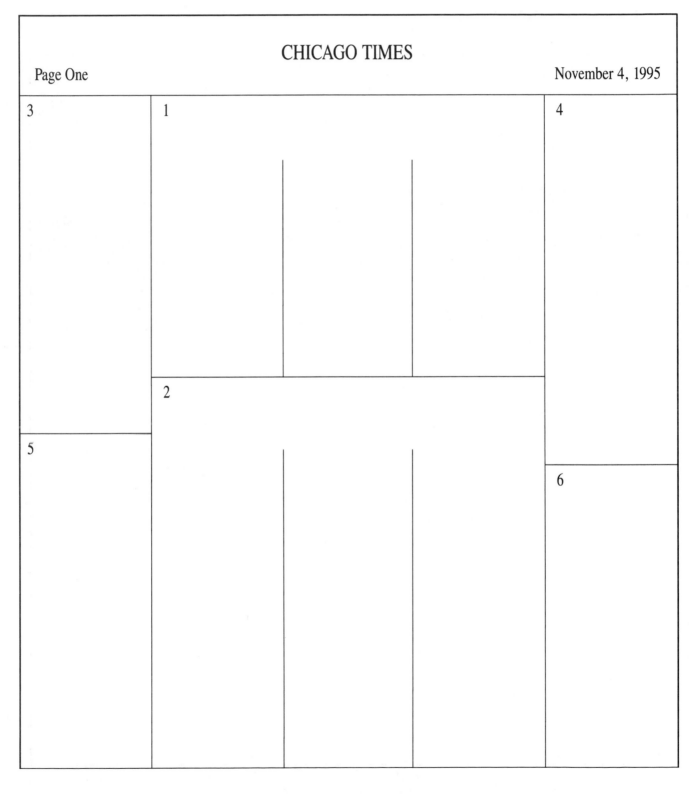

CHICAGO TIMES

Page One   November 4, 1995

3

1

4

2

5

6

B. Put six headlines on this page (design the layout):

Page Two: CHICAGO TIMES, November 4, 1995

C. Write down the four headlines you did not use. Explain why you did not choose them.

1. _____   Reason: _____

   _____   _____

2. _____   Reason: _____

   _____   _____

3. _____   Reason: _____

   _____   _____

4. _____   Reason: _____

   _____   _____

Discuss

Verbally compare your decisions with those of your classmates in your discussion group. Listen carefully. What kinds of stories are important to the people in your group? Explain your opinions. Finally, the group needs to agree on its decisions. One person in the group should write down the group's decision.

Extend

From your experience with the *Chicago Times*, make a one-page newspaper about your class, your university, or your English program. Choose four news stories (three small, one big). Get the information, *write the stories*, and put them on a page. Use a local newspaper to help you.

Who Will Be the Best Teacher?

Vocabulary

advertise to call attention to
minimum the least
requirement something necessary
experience previous work
apply for a job to ask for a job

encourage to suggest strongly
society people living in the
   same way
career profession, life work
hire to give a job to someone

Read and Consider

Last month, one of the best teachers at the Flagstaff (Arizona) Elementary School left his job. The teacher taught science and mathematics.

In June, the school committee advertised the job in Arizona newspapers. Over 100 people applied for the job; the committee chose five possible people for the position.

You are members of the school board. Choose one teacher for the position (and second, third, fourth, and fifth choices).

Decide and Write

Applicant: **Mary Johnstone**, age 24, married (no children)
Qualifications: (1) M.S. degree in mathematics, Stanford University (1990). (2) Two years' teaching experience at elementary school in San Diego, California.
Statement: "I want to return to my home state of Arizona. I love children, and I think science and mathematics are the most important subjects in school."

Reasons to hire: _____

_____

Reasons not to hire: _____

_____

Applicant: **James Fowler**, age 46, married (three children)
Qualifications: (1) M.S. Degree in chemistry, Arizona State University (1968). (2) Twenty-two years' teaching experience at high school in Tucson, Arizona.
Statement: "I don't want to teach high school anymore. I want to teach elementary school. I have three children, and I know the importance of a good elementary education."

Reasons to hire: _____

_____

Reasons not to hire: _____

_____

Applicant: **Barbara Carrera**, age 31, married (four children)
Qualifications: (1) M.S. degree in science education, Gila Bend Community College, Arizona (1982). (2) Two years' teaching experience at elementary school in Gila Bend, Arizona.
Statement: "I love to teach elementary school. Last year, my husband changed his job, and we moved to Flagstaff. I need a job to help the family income."

Reasons to hire: _____

_____

Reasons not to hire: _____

_____

Applicant: **John Jefferson**, age 42, married (one child)
Qualifications: (1) M.S. degree in nutrition, Harvard University (1972). (2) Ten years' teaching experience at University of Nebraska; five years' teaching experience at elementary school in Houston, Texas; five years' teaching experience at elementary school in Albuquerque, New Mexico.
Statement: "Our country needs many more scientists. I will encourage young students to have a scientific career. I think Flagstaff is beautiful!"

Reasons to hire: _____

_____

Reasons not to hire: _____

_____

Applicant: **Judith Jones**, age 27, married (one child)
Qualifications: (1) M.S. degree in biology, Texas Christian University (1986). (2) Four years' teaching experience at elementary school in Lubbock, Texas.
Statement: "A teacher must be strong in the classroom! Most teachers today are too easy. I will teach math and science, and I will tell the students how religion is very important in my personal actions."

Reasons to hire: _____

_____

Reasons not to hire: _____

_____

Our first choice for the job: _____

Second choice: _____

Third choice: _____

Fourth choice: _____

Fifth choice: _____

Discuss

Verbally compare your decisions with those of your classmates in your discussion group. Listen carefully. Has anyone in your group ever had a wonderful (or terrible) teacher? Explain your opinions. Finally, the group needs to agree on its decisions. One person in the group should write down the group's decision.

Extend

1. Do men or do women make better elementary teachers? high school teachers? university professors?

2. Who was your best teacher? Write three reasons why he or she was good.

3. Who was your worst teacher? Why was he or she so bad?

4. Would you like to be a teacher? Explain.

5. How important are teachers to a society?

The Future: What Will Happen If?

Vocabulary

predict to tell about the future
pornography sexual writings/
   pictures

test tube glass container
planet a body in space

Read and Consider

You are a group of writers. You work for the Foretell Corporation. Your corporation predicts the future. You sell your predictions to businesses and organizations.

   Yesterday the Massachusetts Society of Thinkers gave Foretell a list of 12 questions. Your group must answer those questions. Use opinions, facts, and examples in your answers.

Decide and Write

1. What will happen if there is no TV?

   a. _____

   b. _____

   c. _____

2. What will happen if marijuana is legal everywhere in the world?

   a. _____

   b. _____

3. What will happen if all babies are born in test tubes?

   a. _____

   b. _____

4. What will happen if scientists find life on other planets?

   a. _____

   b. _____

5. What will happen if every government leader is a woman?

   a. _____

   b. _____

6. What will happen if there is no more oil in the world?

   a. _____

   b. _____

   c. _____

7. What will happen if there are no laws against pornography?

   a. _____

   b. _____

8. What will happen if scientists prove there is a God?

   a. _____

   b. _____

9. What will happen if computers replace teachers?

   a. _____

   b. _____

10. What will happen if AIDS continues to spread?

     a. _____

     b. _____

11. What will happen if Chinese becomes the international language of the world?

     a. _____

     b. _____

12. What will happen if the world's population continues to increase rapidly?

     a. _____

     b. _____

Summary: Review the 12 questions. Which changes will be good?

Discuss

Verbally compare your decisions with those of your classmates in your discussion group. Listen carefully. What disagreements do people in your group have? Explain your opinions. Finally, the group needs to agree on its decisions. One person in the group should write down the group's decision.

Extend

1. Albert Einstein predicted that people will fight the Fourth World War "with sticks and stones." What did he mean?

2. As the U.S.A. and the U.S.S.R. become weak, which countries will take their places?

3. All living things are changing. What will a human look like in 1 million years? Draw a picture.

4. Will life in the future be better than life now? Explain.

5. Write a composition about the future of your country.

Mikhail Baryshnikov

Jonas Salk

Margaret Thatcher

Kareem Abdul-Jabbar

Which People Should We Clone?

Vocabulary

artificial   not natural; man-made
cell   smallest part of a living thing
organism   any living thing; a plant or an animal

secret   not public; very private
laboratory   place for scientific work
vaccine   liquid that stops a disease

Read and Consider

You are scientists in a secret American science laboratory. For years, you have worked on cloning. In cloning, you take one cell from an organism and make another organism exactly like the first.

For thousands of years, people have cloned plants. In the 1950s, scientists at the Institute for Cancer Research in Philadelphia, Pennsylvania, successfully cloned frogs. In the 1970s, scientists at Oxford and Yale successfully cloned rabbits and mice.

Last week you discovered a way to clone humans. For this to work, the cell must come from someone alive. Whom should you clone?

Carefully consider the effects on society of cloning different people. The following is a list of possibilities. Choose at least five people not on the list.

People from the Arts

Zubin Mehta, conductor
Mikhail Baryshnikov, dancer
Sylvester Stallone, actor
Yo-Yo Ma, musician
Gabriel Garcia Marquez, writer
Placido Domingo, opera singer
Itzhak Perlman, musician
Julio Iglesias, singer
Leonard Bernstein, conductor

Tom Cruise, actor
Madonna, singer
Sonia Braggi, actress
Joan Miro, painter
Eddie Murphy, actor
Aleksandr Solzhenitsyn, writer
Mikis Theodorakis, composer
Liv Ullman, actress

People from Politics/Religion

Margaret Thatcher
Lech Walesa
Desmond Tutu
Oscar Arias

Mikhail Gorbachev
Natan Scharansky
Moammar Qaddafi
Pope John Paul II

People from Sports

Maradona
Steffi Graf
Ben Johnson
Florence Joyner
Jackie Kersey

Carl Lewis
Kareem Abdul-Jabbar
Pele
Michael Jordan
Saduharu Oh

People from the Sciences

Francis Crick, discoverer of DNA, Nobel prize winner
Michael Debakey, heart doctor, developer of artificial heart
Leo Esaki, Nobel prize winner for electron studies
Linus Pauling, Nobel prize winner for atomic studies
Sally Ride, U.S. astronaut
Jonas Salk, virologist, developer of polio vaccine
James Watson, discoverer of DNA, Nobel prize winner
Stephen Hawking, physicist/astronomer, discoverer of black holes

Decide and Write

Choose three people from the *arts*:

Person 1: _____ Reasons: _____

_____

Person 2: _____ Reasons: _____

_____

Person 3: _____ Reasons: _____

_____

Choose three people from the *sciences*:

Person 4: _____ Reasons: _____

_____

Person 5: _____ Reasons: _____

_____

Person 6: _____ Reasons: _____

_____

Choose four people from the fields of *politics, religion, philosophy, sports,* or any other area:

Person 7: _____ Reasons: _____

_____

Person 8: _____ Reasons: _____

_____

Person 9: _____ Reasons: _____

_____

Person 10: _____ Reasons: _____

_____

Discuss

Verbally compare your decisions with those of your classmates in your discussion group. Listen carefully. Support your opinions with examples and facts. Finally, the group needs to agree on its decisions. One person in the group should write down the group's decision.

Extend

1. Who should make decisions about cloning: government leaders? religious people? scientists? others?

2. Will cloning make the world better, or worse? Will the world be better if we have 1000 Einsteins?

3. Before cloning, what was the most important medical discovery?

4. Name five people you would never clone. Explain.

Which Daycare Should We Choose?

Vocabulary

spouse   person your are married to   **snack**   food between meals

Read and Consider

You know a couple that arrived in the United States in Austin, Texas, nine months ago. They have two small children (a 2-year-old boy, and a 3½-year-old girl). At first, only the husband worked (7 A.M. to 5 P.M., $1400/month) in a paper company. At that time, the wife stayed home with the children all day.

However, they have barely enough money to survive. Last week, the wife was offered a job at a bookstore. In fact, the person at the bookstore said she could work part-time (7:30 A.M. to 12:30 P.M., $500/month) or full-time (7:30 A.M. to 5:30 P.M., $1300/month with health benefits). The husband wants the wife to take the full-time job, but the wife is not sure she wants to leave the children for such a long time.

The four childcare facilities in your area (listed on the next page) have openings.

1. Austin Parents Nursery School (APNS):
Times: Morning only 7:45–12:45
Number of children/teachers: 34/2
Cost: $100 per month (per child)
Other features: Lunch provided, parents must participate one morning per week, per child

2. Montessori Country Day School
Times: Full day only 7:30–5:30
Number of children/teachers: 45/6
Cost: $345 per month (per child)
Other features: Lunch and snacks provided

3. Tender Learning Care School
Times: Morning only 7:30–12:00
Number of children/teachers: 17/1
Cost: $180 per month (per child)
Other features: Morning snack provided

4. Merryhill Country School
Times: Full day only 6:30 A.M. to 6:00 P.M.
Number of children/teachers: 23/4
Cost: $300 per month (two children $500)
Other features: Snacks and lunch provided

Decide and Write

In the spaces below, make four possible plans for the couple to follow.

Plan 1:

Will the wife work part-time or full-time? _____

Which daycare will the children attend? _____

_____

Why did you decide this? _____

_____

Plan 2:

Will the wife work part-time or full-time? _____

Which daycare will the children attend? _____

_____

Why did you decide this? _____

_____

Plan 3:

Will the wife work part-time or full-time? _____

Which daycare will the children attend? _____

_____

Why did you decide this? _____

_____

Plan 4 (you make this plan completely yourself):

_____

_____

_____

_____

_____

_____

Discuss

Verbally compare your plan with those of your classmates in your discussion group. How did they decide on part-time or full-time? How did they choose the right daycare? Reach a decision as a group as to the best three plans for the couple to follow.

Extend

1. Is it necessary for a mother to stay home with young children? If no, why not? If yes, why and until what age?

2. How would you feel if the father rather than the mother stayed home with the children?

3. When you were a child, how did your parents take care of you from birth to five years old? Do you think they would do the same today?

4. Aside from time, cost, teacher/children ratio, what are important factors to consider when choosing a good daycare facility?

How Do We Change the World?

Vocabulary

system items connected to make a whole

accept to agree to

reject to refuse

communism, socialism, capitalism economic systems

constitution written statement of laws or ideas for a government

representative one who acts for other people

entire all

Read and Consider

United Nations Resolution 4789   June 6, 2075

The world has many problems. The Second World War was from 1940–1945; the Third World War was from 1998–2000; the Fourth World War was from 2036–2041; and the Fifth World War (2064–2074) ended last year.

Obviously, it is time to change the system of world politics. The biggest problem is the large number of countries in the world. Because of nationalism, the government of each country only wants to do good things for its own country. As a result, the people of the world fight and kill each other.

All the countries in the world now want a new world government; we will choose a special United Nations Commission to suggest ways of remaking the world!

You are members of the special U.N. Commission.

Decide and Write

A. Look at a world map. Divide the world into three regions. Name each region.

B. Capitals: Choose one capital for the world and one capital for each region.

Main world capital: _____

Reason: _____

Regional capital of _____ (name of region): _____

Reason: _____

Regional capital of _____ (name of region): _____

Reason: _____

Regional capital of _____ (name of region): _____

Reason: _____

C. Type of government. Choose one; put a check mark by it.

_____ 1. No president, a General Assembly with one representative from each country (we have that now). The entire group of representatives will make all decisions.

_____ 2. No president, a General Assembly with one representative from each country (we have that now). The General Assembly will choose a special group to make all decisions.

_____ 3. A General Assembly with one representative from each country (we have that now). The General Assembly chooses a president every two years. The president and General Assembly make important decisions.

_____ 4. (a different plan) _____

_____

_____

_____

Reason for your choice: _____

_____

_____

_____

D. Economic system. Choose one; put a check mark by it.

_____ Communism   _____ Socialism   _____ Capitalism

_____ (different system) _____

Reasons for your choice: _____

_____

_____

E. A flag. Draw a flag for the new world government:

What does the flag represent? _____

_____

F. Language. Choose two official languages:

Main language: _____   Second language: _____

Reason: _____

Discuss

Verbally compare your decisions with those of your classmates in your discussion group. Listen carefully, and explain your opinions. Finally, the group needs to agree on its decisions. One person in the group should write down its decision.

Extend

Ask at least three people inside your class these questions. Write a short paragraph summarizing the results.

	Yes	No	Undecided

1. Should everyone in the new world speak the same language?   _____ _____ _____

Reasons: _____

_____

2. Should there be one religion in the world?   _____ _____ _____

Reasons: _____

_____

3. Should there be one kind of world money?   _____ _____ _____

Reasons: _____

_____

4. Would the world be better with no
   countries?   _____   _____   _____

   Reasons: _____

   _____

5. Should the educational system be
   public, or private?   _____   _____   _____

   Reasons: _____

   _____

What Do Men and Women Think About Love?

Vocabulary

popular   liked by many people
questionnaire   list of questions
dating   asking and going out with
   someone of the opposite sex

personality   qualities of a person
opinion   personal belief

Read and Consider

People is a popular magazine. Every month it has information for women and men.

You are editors of *People*. Next month you are going to put a questionnaire in the magazine. The questionnaire will ask men and women for their opinions about love. Your job is to write the questionnaire.

Decide and Write

This Year's *People* Dating Questionnaire!

1. (Example) How do you know when you are in love?

   Answer: _____

   _____

2. Question: _____

   _____

   Answer: _____

   _____

3. Question: _____

   _____

   Answer: _____

   _____

4. Question: _____

   _____

   Answer: _____

   _____

5. Question: _____

   _____

   Answer: _____

   _____

6. Question: _____

_____

Answer: _____

_____

7. Question: _____

_____

Answer: _____

_____

8. Question: _____

_____

Answer: _____

_____

9. Question: _____

_____

Answer: _____

_____

10. Question: _____

_____

Answer: _____

_____

11. Question: _____

     _____

     Answer: _____

     _____

12. Question: _____

     _____

     Answer: _____

     _____

13. Question: _____

     _____

     Answer: _____

     _____

14. Question: _____

     _____

     Answer: _____

     _____

15. Question: In the movie *Love Story*, one character said, ''Love means that you never have to say you are sorry.'' Do you agree? Explain.

     Answer: _____

     _____

Discuss

Verbally compare your decisions with those of your classmates in your discussion group. Listen carefully. Explain your opinions. Have you or your classmates ever been in love? Finally, the group needs to agree on its decisions. One person in the group should write down the group's decision.

Extend

Ask your questions of at least three of your classmates. Then ask your questions of at least three people outside your class (Americans, if possible). Compare and discuss the results in class.

The People Are Poor: How Do We Help Them?

Vocabulary

welfare   free money from government

poverty   poorness

Read and Consider

Most of the people in your country are poor. Many of these poor people are unemployed and homeless. You are members of the GCHP (Government Commission to Help the Poor). You have a budget of $5 million. Study the following information. How can you help the poor people?

Group	A	B	C	D	E
Annual income	$100,000+	$20,000+	$7,500+	$2,000+	$0+
Total population	20,000	62,500	145,000	213,000	221,000
Homeless	0	0	5,000	30,000	73,000
Unemployed (%)	0%	0%	3%	45%	100%
Monthly food expense	$2,000	$750	$250	$150	$50 (welfare)

Total population: 661,500
Poverty line: $7,500
Poor people: 452,000 (68%)
Birthrate: 7.5 children per family

Income tax: none
Businesses: 19,500
Business tax: 2% of profits
   (20 million/year)

Decide and Write

Rank the following in order of importance (1 = most important, 7 = least important):

_____ Find jobs for unemployed.

_____ Give food to people in Group E.

_____ Build low-cost apartments for homeless.

_____ Decrease birthrate.

_____ Increase welfare.

_____ Increase taxes for people.

_____ Increase taxes for business.

Area 1: **Welfare**
How much money should the government give to each poor person?

Group D: _____   Group E: _____

How much tax should the other people pay for the welfare ($ per family per year)?

Group A: _____   Group B: _____   Group C: _____

Area 2: **Jobs**
How can the unemployed people in classes C, D, E get a job?

1. _____

2. _____

3. _____

Area 3: **Housing**
How many apartments should the government build for the poor people?

	This Year	*Next Year*
Group E:	_____	_____
Group F:	_____	_____

Area 4: **Population**
How can the government lower the birthrate?

1. _____

2. _____

3. _____

Area 5: **Food**
How can the government get food to the poor people?

1. _____

2. _____

3. _____

Discuss

Verbally compare your decisions with those of your classmates in your discussion group. Listen carefully. Explain your opinions. What is the best way to help poor people? Finally, the group needs to agree on its decisions. One person in the group should write down the group's decision.

Extend

1. Do you agree or disagree (explain)?
    a. Most poor people are lazy.
    b. Most poor people are uneducated.
    c. Most poor people spend their money carefully.
    d. The government has a responsibility to help poor people.

2. What are the main causes of poverty?

3. Write a composition describing the situation of poor people in your country.

The Greenhouse Effect: What Should We Do?

Vocabulary

chlorofluorocarbons gases   **prohibit** forbid

Read and Consider

The world is getting hotter. During the 1980s, the average world temperature increased by three degrees. The hottest three years in the last century were 1987, 1988, and 1989. The temperature is increasing because of the *greenhouse effect*. Carbon dioxide (CO_2) and chlorofluorocarbons are increasing in the atmosphere. Less heat is escaping from the Earth.

Scientists predict that the world's temperature will rise ten more degrees by the year 2025. Many parts of the world may become deserts. There might be much less food and water for the people in the world.

You are members of an international congress of scientists and politicians. What should you do about each of the following problems?

Decide and Write

Problem A: **Forests**
Trees use carbon dioxide to produce oxygen. Unfortunately, people are destroying trees and forests all over the world. For example, over 2000 acres of Brazilian rainforest (the largest forest in the world) are cut down every day so that people can use the land.

Recommendations: 1. _____

_____

_____

2. _____

_____

_____

Problem B: **Chlorofluorocarbons**
Every time a person turns on an air conditioner or uses a spray deodorant, these gases go into the air. These gases combine with CO_2 to hold heat.

Recommendations: 1. _____

_____

_____

2. _____

_____

_____

Problem C: **Motor Vehicles**
Most of the carbon dioxide is produced when a fossil fuel (oil, coal, gas) burns. There are over 2 billion cars, trucks, buses, airplanes, and trains in the world that run on gasoline.

Recommendations: 1. _____

_____

_____

2. _____

_____

_____

Problem D: **Factories and Plants**

Many factories and plants that produce electricity and other products use coal for power.

Recommendations: 1. _____

_____

_____

2. _____

_____

_____

Problem E: **Education**

Most people in the world don't know about the greenhouse effect.

Recommendations: 1. _____

_____

_____

2. _____

_____

_____

The congress will now vote on the following ideas:

Yes   *No*

_____   _____   1. Each family (five people) can have only one car.

_____   _____   2. Air conditioning in houses and cars should be prohibited.

_____   _____   3. More nuclear power plants should be built.

_____   _____   4. Buses should be completely replaced by electric-powered trains.

_____   _____   5. Brazil cannot destroy any more forests.

_____   _____   6. Each car can have only ten gallons of gasoline per month.

_____   _____   7. All oil production should be reduced by 50%.

_____   _____   8. A worldwide limit of two children per family should be enforced (to stop development of land).

_____   _____   9. Each country must plant trees on 5% of its land.

_____   _____   10. All electrical plants that use coal or gas must be closed.

_____   _____   11. All new houses must use solar energy.

_____   _____   12. All production of cars, trucks, buses, and airplanes should be stopped for one year.

_____   _____   13. The world should make a permanent organization to analyze the greenhouse effect.

Discuss

Verbally compare your decisions with those of your classmates in your discussion group. Listen carefully; what do your classmates think? Explain your opinions. Finally, the group needs to agree on its decisions. One person in the group should write down the group's decision.

Extend

Write a composition about how the greenhouse effect might change the way you live (your personal life).

Cave In: Who Will Get Out Alive?

Vocabulary

miner underground worker

cave large hole inside the Earth

Read and Consider

You are a group of Brazilian miners. Last night you were working in a diamond cave 500 meters below ground. Suddenly, one of the walls fell in! Now you cannot get out. But rescuers can talk to you with a radio.

Fortunately, the rescuers are going to dig a small hole to the cave in about 30 minutes. The hole will be big enough for one person to get through at a time.

But the hole will be very weak. After one or two of you gets through the hole it probably will fall in! *After that, no more rescue will be possible. Everyone in the cave will die.* You must decide who will get out of the hole. Consider that:

The first person through the hole will live.

The second person through the hole probably will live.

The third person through the hole will have a 50/50 chance.

The fourth person through the hole probably will die.

The fifth (sixth, etc.) person through the hole will die.

Also, think of five different orders for people to go out the hole.

Decide and Write

                        Name   *Age*

1. Basis of Order: <u>(Example) Age: Youngest to Oldest</u>

    First person out: _____ _____

                     _____ _____

                     _____ _____

    Last person out: _____ _____

2. Basis of order: _____

    First person out: _____ _____

                     _____ _____

                     _____ _____

    Last person out: _____ _____

3. Basis of order: _____

    First person out: _____ _____

                     _____ _____

                     _____ _____

    Last person out: _____ _____

4. Basis of order: _____

    First person out: _____ _____

                     _____ _____

                     _____ _____

    Last person out: _____ _____

5. Basis of order: _____

   First person out: _____ _____

   _____ _____

   _____ _____

   Last person out: _____ _____

Which is the best order to solve the problem?

_____

Discuss

Verbally compare your decisions with those of your classmates in your discussion group. Listen carefully; be sure to give reasons to put yourself in the position of "First person out." Finally, the group needs to agree on its decisions. One person in the group should write down the group's decision.

Extend

1. If you are part of a group that is in the mine, will you accept a group decision that you must die?

2. If you knew you were going to die next week, what would you do tomorrow?

3. Do you think there is life after death? Explain.

4. What is the most important thing for a person to do in his or her life?